DEDICATED TO ALL WHO SERVED AND DIED FOR OUR FREEDOM

While America was Sleeping

by

Roger L. Bilbrey

© Copyright 2020 – Roger L. Bilbrey
Tree of Life Coaching
ISBN: 978-1-7332018-4-1

Printed in the United States of America
Roger Bilbrey & Associates---Publisher

Edited Version

WWW.TREEOFLIFECOACHING.ORG

TABLE OF CONTENTS

    The African American Civil Rights Movements
    Major movements from the '50s- the '70s
    The Gay Civil Rights Movement
    The Counterculture Movement
    Black Lives Matter Movement
    ANTIFA

Introduction

A while back, I woke up with an unrest in my soul. Since that time, I haven't been able to shake it, nor do I ever want to.

I saw what best could be described as a vision of something that is about to take place in America. I don't know if we can change the events or not. It may be too late. However, I believe we need to get the word out and heed the warnings.

When I have shared my heart about this with others, I was shocked to find that they too had this unrest in their souls and an overwhelming emergency to get the word out, NOW!!!! I wanted to get this book out while I still have the freedom to do so. I fear freedom is soon going to be taken away and the plan is already in the works to stop our freedom of speech as well as thought.

Please understand, I am not an alarmist, I am not a person who believes in unfounded conspiracies, nor do I fear what may be the outcome of sharing this story, should anyone attempt to silence me. As Patrick Henry once said, "Give me Liberty or give me death!" I would personally rather be long gone than to have my freedoms, and those of my family and friends taken away.

You may not think that taking a person's life or torture would ever happen in America just because someone is voicing his opinion. But, in many countries around the world, they never believed it would happen to them either, untill it did!!!

There is a force within this country that hates America's long-standing tradition of values and wants to destroy everything that makes, and has made, America great.

I will be making statements that some of our leaders have made, and why we should be concerned. I am not going to try and persuade you to vote for either side. As a matter of fact, based on some of the studies I will point out, you might be shocked at just how little our leaders can do to make a difference.

I do believe that while we have the freedom and chance to vote, we should do so, and do it with the conviction of our values, instead of what freebies they are offering for their votes.

I will be talking about four steps that have been placed in our society years ago that have helped bring this once young and robust nation, to a nation that even the smallest enemies now no longer fear.

I will try and explain why our money is to the point of worthlessness, why our kids are doing what they are doing and why the country seems not to be able to determine right from wrong.

I will try and explain why the church no longer has the transforming power it once had, and why most people now make fun of what believers deem most holy.

I want to say first and foremost that I love my God with all that is within me and want to have the rights that America, when founded, gave me to worship Him in the way I see fit.

I want to say secondly that I love my family, and I love America with all that is within me. I am willing to die for any of these so that future Americans can enjoy what I have enjoyed for over 60 years. It has once been said that anything good is worth fighting for, and I believe these are an excellent top three.

We now have a generation that has no idea the cost of the freedom we have in America. We live in a time when we have more than we have ever had, yet are more dissatisfied as well.

The America that I see today is nowhere near the America that I knew as a young man. We have conformed so much that America is known to most of the world as a nation of gluttons and bullies. We are no longer looked upon with respect.

This didn't happen overnight. The way that America is today and the direction she is heading is happening for a reason. All the violence, division, hatred, economic woes, and more, have been placed in our society by individuals who want to take us over.

They have used our problems we face in America as a sounding board to push their agenda even though they know full well, the program they want to put in place will not help, but further make the problems much worse. It has all been done, "While America was Sleeping."

Is there a solution to the problem? Let's dig in and find out.....

Chapter 1

A LETTER FROM AMERICA'S FUTURE

To whoever finds this:

I am writing this letter to anyone who may find it. The only way I felt safe to get my information out is by letter and not signing it. There are guards, cameras, and microphones everywhere. Even our televisions now have cameras that are recording everything said and done in our homes.

I am so fearful of writing down these words, fearful that if I am caught doing so, my life will be taken or that I might be cast into prison. But I have to try and relieve the pressure to voice my opinions on what has happened to America.

I never in a million years would have ever dreamt this great nation of America would fall so profoundly so soon. It seems like only yesterday I was a boy riding my bike in my neighborhood with other children.

I remember not having air conditioning, so we would raise our windows at night and turn on a fan to let in the fresh air. We didn't even lock our doors as we knew everyone on the block, and never was there a reason for fear.

The television shows I watched all had a wholesome valuable lesson to be learned. I did see how they were trying to slip things in, but not in a bold manner. My parents told me that before I came along, even characters playing mother and father roles had to be in separate beds, and if they were in one bed, each had to have one foot on the floor. But slowly, the movie industry was broadening its message of inclusion versus values.

It was very subtle at the start. It started with families with only one parent, a cartoon of a woman living with seven dwarfs, getting the lone ranger hero to remove his mask, all done in such a fashion to not alarm us or make us uncomfortable.

Before long, there would be more violence and less good heroes. Then comedians began making fun of the God which our nation was founded upon.

There is no respect for law enforcement, preachers, our nation, or even parents anymore. We have pro athletes who refuse to stand in honor of our country and what it represents, and we feel it's ok because of a small amount of what they call an injustice.

Now, at the time of writing this letter, even our leaders of this country make fun of God or anyone who believes in Him. They also mock our flag and patriotism as something to be ashamed of.

Speaking of politicians, I remember how they would talk about God and love of country and what they were going to do for our country. Now, they no longer tell what they plan on doing for our country but what the opposing candidate has done that should disqualify them from being president. And the things that we once stood up and fought for, such as the right for a baby in the womb to live, they will boldly say that it's ok to kill them because it is the mother's right.

On the local news, they made it seem that everyone was in agreement on the abortion law. They used the same propaganda to make us believe that the church was a hate group and that capitalism was nothing but selfishness and should be done away with.

They told us lies about moral leaders so that we wouldn't elect them or vote them into a position of power such as a supreme court judge. We got to where we didn't know who was telling the truth anymore.

It has only been three years since our last election. They promised us free health care, free schooling, and canceling school debts. They talked of making sure everyone's rights would be protected, especially gays, illegals, and others. They told us they were going to fix the gun violence to where we would never have to worry about that again.

All of this sounded so good to me. Who wouldn't want free health care and schooling? Who wouldn't want everyone to have the freedom to do as they pleased? And finally, it seemed, we could have the comfort of safety like I once knew as a child, knowing the government was protecting us against violent armed people.

I was the first to be in the poll line to vote for my candidate, who stood for all these things. And my candidate won! Now to my shock and disbelief, I may never have the right to vote again. They lied! It was all just a lie to get our votes and their hidden agenda in.

I remember my father telling me as a boy how evil communistic and socialistic views were. He warned me of the lies they would speak to get into position and then take control of everything the citizens held dear. I passed it off as him being old-fashioned, out-dated, and not progressive in his thinking. Oh, how I wish I had listened to him.

This last election, our country finally accepted and trusted in the socialism belief and voted a communist as our president.

For the first couple of years, things appeared to be great, and everyone had hope that America was again a great, caring, peaceful country. We now had free health care and schools. No one had guns anymore, so we felt safe. Guards from the U.N. surrounded every block, they said to protect us.

But toward the end of the second year of their victory at the polls, I noticed our healthcare was becoming worse with each passing day. Our school system was told what they could and couldn't say. Our churches were being under attack with doors closing. The only ones that were able to stay open were the ones that were willing to preach what the government allowed them to say. And for the record, it was against everything this nation once stood for, or for that matter, what God stood for.

You might wonder why people didn't have guns. It is because our government made all it's citizens surrender them. I remember before they took them, my friends said they would die with their guns in their hands before giving up their arms. However, that wasn't the case. No one in all of America fought to keep their firearms. Government troops moved into every neighborhood with tanks ready to blow up anyone's home that refused to hand over their guns.

They even went to the schools and took our children hostage and said they would kill them if we didn't surrender our weapons. Not one person fought against the government. Not one!

The moment our weapons were taken, the government became very bold in showing all of the American citizens that they were now in control, not " we the people."

With no way to defend ourselves, we were left to their mercy. It wasn't until that time that I studied and found out why our forefathers gave us the right to bear arms. It wasn't to protect our family; it was to protect ourselves from any government that might try and take us over, even our own!

Now they are in full control. They tell us where we will work. They tell us how long we will work and how much we will be paid (which is very little). Those of us who owned anything, it was taken away and given to others that didn't have as much.

Not only do they kill children being born at will, but if you get too sick or old to work, you will be annihilated as well.

If you try and do anything that is against the government, even as little as a small prayer meeting, your neighbors will tell on you because of fear not to tell.

Without our weapons, no one is willing to resist. We follow their agenda as sheep going to the slaughter. They take our hard-earned money and disperse some to more unfortunate people, but most of it, they keep for themselves. If anyone speaks against them in any way, they are sent to prison or shot on the spot.

The people in the entertainment business and the civil rights movements they used to get their message across were killed as soon as they took over. They have also taken over every broadcast news so they can promote their agenda and hide the actual facts of their tyranny.

We feel hopeless and fearful. No longer is America the land of the free. It is now a land that is controlled by a dictator. The leaders seem to hate the old America and all the values it once held dear. Why did they come to America to begin with then? There were plenty of other countries like the way they have transformed ours.

I fear for my kids and grandkids. How will they survive such a brutal and ruthless government as the one we have now? Every night I pray that someone, or a group of people, will find a way to take back our country, but how can they?

I don't know what this letter can do should someone find it. Most likely, nothing. But I hope for a miracle that will change the position that we find ourselves in today. The place that we so foolishly voted for when we had the right to vote.

I plead with anyone who may find this letter that if you have a government like America once had, take the words of a fool and never take that freedom for granted and fight for it with all you have, or you will be doomed for the same fate as us.

Chapter 2

D-DAY, THE BEGINNING OF AN END

The first chapter was written in fiction form, but sadly, a good bit of what was said is real today, and I believe if we continue in that path, we will find it all to be true. And for the record, this is the first time in my life that I genuinely fear my own government.

I will be repeating some of the things in the first chapter that are true now to show how far we have moved into this new way of thinking that will, if left unchecked, destroy our nation.

There is a plan to take over America, to take the freedom we hold dear, and to change our form of democratic governance to a socialist government. We need to wake up and turn the tide before it's too late.

The story told next are actual events. It was a bleak time in our nation's history, but it will be far worse if we continue to march to the lies of socialism.

It started out like any other Sunday. All over America, people were sleeping in, while others were getting ready for church, family outings, and such.

Not as many people as today were getting ready for work, because, in most states, the businesses were under what was called "the Blue Law" which made many companies not able to open because Sunday was considered God's day.

America felt safe and secure, no reason for alarm. Things appeared to be going great. It was so secure that the military personnel were given passes to go to church that day.

Then out of nowhere, there appeared two blips on a radar screen at 7:02 AM. Just 53 minutes later, all hell broke loose. Bombers were everywhere. American military fighters were scrambling to get what was left of the planes up in the air to fight against the foe that had surprisingly attacked us.

Never before, since Britain tried to take us over, has another country had the nerve to try and start a war with us on American soil.

At that point in time, America was a country with enormous power, economics, influence, and respect from other countries. All countries, including other countries that were almost as powerful as us, were afraid to take on such actions as did Japan on that day.

The powers that be knew there was a potential problem like this, but no actions were taken to secure our nation.

The date was Dec 7, 1941, the place, Pearl Harbor. As the president said the day after, "Yesterday, Dec. 7, 1941, a date which will live in infamy, the United States of America was suddenly and deliberately attacked by naval and air forces of the Empire of Japan."

Indeed the haunting words spoken by the president have rung loud throughout the years of a young America, "A date which will live in infamy." But this will fail in comparison to the danger that America is beginning to face, not from enemies from another land coming to America to fight, but enemies from within the United States that are determined to take us over.

I remember the days of my childhood. Being born in the '50s, things were calm. Many people attended church. We felt so safe; we didn't even lock our doors and, as a matter of fact, kept our windows cracked for air while we slept at night since most homes didn't have air conditioning.

You could let your children watch TV unattended because you knew nothing would come on the air that would destroy the values you have taught them. If anything did try to slip in, there would be such an outcry from the public that whoever had tried to do so would be put out of business.

Most all the shows back then consisted of families, meaning father, mother, and children. I had to make the statement what family meant for this generation, as the Supreme Court of the land is trying hard to figure out what the meaning of family is supposed to be, even as this part of the book is being written.

Not only did the shows depict functional families, but they also had a moral message and teaching in the scripted lines that children could live by for the most part.

The biggest problems the schools had mainly were children chewing gum, talking in class, and throwing paper. I know some of you use Snoop to find your answers, but I know that this statement above, although not proven when it was first said, was true because in the '60s I was in school, and I personally saw those to be the biggest problems.

But slowly and secretly, things were changing. People's views of God, our freedoms and rights, and our long-standing fundamentals of the way our government was formed were being challenged.

By the '60s, prayer was taken out of school, young people were practicing "free love and taking dope, and God was being pushed out of the equation, who was and is the supreme thing we needed for our survival.

By the '70s, when I was in high school, teachers were beginning to be afraid of the students because of the lack of respect they gave to the teachers. Police encamped around my school after each class ended because of the drugs and fighting. Smoking and drinking among kids became a norm around their peers.

My, how the times have changed. Our money is the weakest around the world than it ever has been. Millions of children are killed each day under the title of abortion. There is no respect for the law, religious leaders, parents, teachers, or government leaders.

Those who believe in God are made fun of and in the minority.

Another enemy attacked our nation on Sept. 11, 2001, and this time, not a specific country, but a group of terrorists with little military weapons or size at that time.

People come to our nation, who have no idea about the cost of our freedom or the understanding of how this nation was formed under the basic principles of the Bible. Illegals are now mostly allowed to stay in our country and use our government programs, thus putting a strain on our economy.

All these things are a plan devised from the beginning to destroy this nation. It is a war being fought within by people who hate us. People who we have trusted and have given the power to change our laws. Russia had made the statement that they would take us over without firing a shot. They were right.

Many people don't believe our government will turn on us, take our guns, our religious freedoms, and our money. That's what the Jews, Germans, Russians, and other countries thought also.

Trust me, we have millions of Americans that would love to see all Christians done away with, and as far as that goes, many of our leaders wish the same.

Americans have sold their birthright as Esau did when he sold his birth right for a little food. They have voted people into office who promise to secure what they thought would save their lives by being promised better jobs, better schools, and sharing more of the good life.

It may already be too late to even vote the right people in. Our voting system can be tampered with, and there is talk of a complete takeover of American. Still, others talk of an elite, wealthy, and powerful group that tells our leaders what they will or will not do.

Our government no longer cares about the will of the people but is fighting hard to take full control of all power, and all this is being done while most Americans are enjoying life, taking it easy, and seeing no danger in sight. We, as a nation, have once again fallen asleep.

Even the church in the midst of all of this has fallen prey. God's people, who are supposed to have the

Holy Spirit and be led by Him, are acting just like the world and have no sense of right or wrong.

You may not be of the Christian faith, but I would hope you will continue to read the rest of this book even though you are not. But the Bible which I have faith in has warned us about this age.

I want to be clear when I make statements like the following. I am not downing any president or any leader in position or running for a seat, but instead just showing the actual results of their actions or the future consequences of their ideas.

That being said, I remember when President Obama was giving his campaign speech and in it made statements like "I am going to bring back the America it once was."

Can I just say, I must not be that old, because I have never seen America as it is today, and frankly, I don't like what I see.

I remember stories told about the 1939 movie "Gone with the Wind." The whole nation got in an uproar because of the statement made by actor Clark Gable that said, "Frankly my dear, I don't give a damn."

For the first time, a curse word was spoken in a public movie. Why was that such a shock? Because in the movie industry of 1930's, their <u>own</u> code prohibited the word "damn" to be used as well as any other profanity.

Since that time, we have songs being played over the radio that make that word sound like a word in a nursery rhyme, and nobody seems to care. Completely nude sexual acts are now being played in prime time right on our home television and computers.

Even now, the famous quote in "Gone with the Wind" was voted the number one movie line of all time by the American Film Institute in 2005. NUMBER 1?!!!! We've come a long way baby.

So how did we get this way?

I am going to expose how our nation and its people have used tactics to bring this nation down. I will go over the basic four tactics that communist parties have used in the past to finally overthrow a country without having to fire a shot. It is through subversion, and it's being used today IN AMERICA and has been for some time now.

Chapter 3

SOCIALISM IS NOT NEW TO AMERICA

In the early 17th century, America was being established as a new country. The founders escaped the rule that Britain had on them to find a place where they could have the freedom to work, prosper, look for gold, and to worship and grow as they pleased.

Although there is a debate on the actual timing, it is mainly believed that starting in the 17th century, capitalism was beginning to form, and by the 19th century, it was the most accepted way.

Many people feel that capitalism was built on the backs of slavery, which may or may not have been an accurate statement. However, today, capitalism is more dependent on who wants to learn and work to get to the place they want to be.

Still, others say that even now, people are getting rich off the backs of others through low wages and hard labor. Here is where I have a problem. Everyone in the 21st century can go to school, start a job, and do as they need to do to make it in life.

You do not have to go to work for someone who pays low and demands hard work for the effort. You have the right and privilege to start your own business, set your own rules, and hire the people you want.

The socialist system sounds good on paper, but in action, it can bring so many problems. One of those is that once many countries start to accept socialism, it soon embraces communism and that usually ends in complete disaster for the country and its people.

You will also notice in this book how both the socialist and the communist points of view use things like job rights, racial rights, and other popular agendas today to further their support regardless if they truly are fighting for these people. It is a tool they use to gain people's trust and to gain people's support.

In the early years of the 20th century, this was proven when the trade unions, people who were part of the progressive reform, immigrants, and others, joined in on the fight to push the socialist agenda. I would love to be able to get into those other groups, but that is not the primary purpose of the book, so we will just skim the surface to show how this socialistic idea has grown in America and where its beginning formed.

T.S. Eliot once said, "Most of the evil in this world is done by people with good intentions."

Socialism is not new to America. In fact, it can be traced as far back as the 1850s! The first that I could find it, started with some immigrant Germans who formed the National Typographic Union in 1852.

From there, it wasn't long till the Socialist Party of America was formed in 1901, which consisted of the democratic socialist and the social-democratic political party in the United States, along with the Social Democratic Party of America and parts of the Socialist Labor Party of America.

Is it any wonder why today, in 2020, there is such a push for socialism in America? Although this book isn't written to bash any particular party, I am just pointing out which party the socialists have been working through for years.

It was shocking to me to find out how early socialism was in America. I also want to point out that socialism and communism are not the same things, but to my surprise, communism has been around about as long as socialism has in America.

By 1919, many of the Socialist Party of America had already left to join the Communist International and from there many others left to join the Communist Party USA.

By 2020, we now have many that are mayors, governors, court leaders, and members of congress that are advocates for socialism, which, as before stated, will eventually turn to communism. Almost half of the population of America is for that idea because they feel that capitalism has failed them.

Are you beginning to see how, when a country begins to embrace these ideologies, it eventually deepens to communism? I highly suggest that you spend some time researching the topic of communism in early America so you can see just how strong it has been all along in our history "While America was Sleeping."

Chapter 4

Phase I -- SUBVERSION

It was said by George Santayana, "Those who cannot learn from history are doomed to repeat it." We can find all kinds of history that prove that socialism and communism are not suitable for a country. The only way it has made it into countries is the constant lies it told the people and by hiding the truth of what was really going on behind the scene. The only way to know what is happening is by having someone who is on the inside who is willing to bring the truth to the forefront.

The information contained here was taken in part by a defected KGB leader named Yuri Bezmenov who witnessed first-hand how communists take over a nation. He tried to warn America in 1983 of the dangers of socialism and communism, but from the looks of what is happening, we didn't listen. Will we listen now?!!!

Let me tell you a little about the history of Bezmenov and why we should listen to his warnings.

He had worked for RIA Novosti, which was and still is a Russian news media organization. As I already mentioned, he was also a KGB agent, who was responsible for gathering information on both internal and foreign affairs for Russia's intelligence. I would imagine it to be similar to our CIA but with much more corruption because of what they would do with the information gathered. However, that being said, we have no idea what our government might be doing with the information they are gathering on us. I think that everything that comes from and to the government should have a check and balance system to help keep it honest. Two eyes are always better than one. And it also should be set up to where neither side would benefit from the other on information or aids it represents.

When Bezmenov worked as a journalist with RIA Novosti, it is interesting to note that about three-fourths of Novosti's staff were KGB officers, and the remaining worked for them at one time or were KGB freelance writers and informers. At that time, Bezmenov also was working for the KGB.

Now is it any wonder that almost all of our news media is controlled by the far-left? And what is the desire of the far-left? To push the American people to a socialist agenda, of course! With no real opposition to that type of reporting, how can we get useful, unbiased news where we can make a conscientious and wise decision on things going on in our country?

As of the time of writing this book, Donald Trump is president and, as far as I am concerned, coined the phrase, "Fake News!" Many people made fun of that statement when he said it, but trust me, the media is not for what this country once stood for and is very biased for the far-left agenda.

Just a side note, in case you haven't realized it by now, media plays a significant role in how a society believes. What we view on the news is how we think our country is heading. If all the news makes it appear that the majority of the country is for socialism, then we begin to believe that it is a fact. Instead, it might just be a small handful of people with a loud voice to be heard. We will talk more about this further along.

Bezmenov wasn't a freelance writer for RIA Novosti, but rather, it was his job to edit what was written and plant propaganda materials that would go to foreign media. He also conducted tours for delegates from other countries, as guests to Novosti, of the Soviet Union and/or to the international conferences that would be held in the Soviet Union.

I remember many years ago of a person who claimed to have had first-hand knowledge of one of those tours to Russia during the communist controlled USSR. He claimed Russia was trying to show us how good communism was for the country.

Sure enough, when they viewed the small area they were allowed to see, the schools, hospitals, department stores, healthcare, and jobs were excellent. Furthermore, all the people in that area were well dressed and appeared to be happy.

Later, according to him, it was revealed through secrecy from a person that lived there, that the government had deceived us. According to the informant, the government had worked on a few city blocks making the buildings look great and supplied top items in hospitals, stores, and more. They also gave people beautiful clothing. However, locals were told not to speak of the truth that was hidden by the false persona. The people were told if they spoke against the system, they would be imprisoned or shot. They also placed guards all around to make sure everything worked as planned.

If this is true, there is no reason why many of the people who are in our government now believe that socialism and communism are such good things. They only saw the façade that Russia wanted them to see.

I don't know if the things said were fact or not, but I do know that I have several family members and friends who have lived in communist countries, including Russia, and they have said that the conditions are horrible. We will go more into how communists try to deceive as we further expose what Novosti tried to warn us about.

Bezmenov said he was forced after several months to be an informer while working his job as a journalist. Through his career and him spreading disinformation to foreign countries, he was able to further his purpose to spread propaganda and subversion.

I gave a background on Bezmenov, to show you that he had first-hand knowledge of communism and its goal. But what is so amazing, you will find out later on in this book, that once you have been indoctrinated in socialism, you still won't believe the truth even though it is right before your eyes.

With that being said, let me first begin by giving you the definition of subversion.

1. the act of subverting: the state of being subverted; especially: a systematic attempt to overthrow or undermine a government or political system by persons working secretly from within
2. Two obsolete: a cause of overthrow or destruction

Once again, in case you haven't noticed thus far, this is precisely what is happening now in our country. We have people in our government, even up to the Senate and House of Representatives, that are working within to overthrow our political and governance system.

We, to my surprise, have people in our Senate and House of Representatives that are openly admitting to being socialist and some even hint at being communist. We have one that has a religion that despises America and, in that religion, has the right to lie and say anything to deceive Americans. That alone shows how far we have come down this road to America's downfall.

For the past several years now, they have passed laws that we the people were against. They do this boldly because they are now in a position where there is no stopping them without a radical movement.

Right has become wrong and wrong right. The values that America once held dear are mocked by those in leadership. Some even believe our constitution and flag are offensive.

How did we get this far? Our forefathers would roll over in their grave if they could see what is going on now. Well, it didn't happen overnight. This hard push to turn our country to socialism has been in the works for a long time now, well over 50 years, and they have used the tactic of subversion to do it.

Isn't it amazing at how much time they are willing to take to change the thinking of a country? Most of the people who helped start this over 50-year program are old or have died since, but they wanted it so bad, they were willing to move as slowly as needed to bring this new agenda to fruition without people even being aware of what is going on. Let's look to see how they use subversion and why it takes so long to work.

The first act that the socialists and communists use in subversion is demoralization. The meaning of demoralization, according to Merriam Webster, is 1. to cause to turn aside or away from what is good or true or morally right; to corrupt the morals of 2. to upset or destroy the normal functioning of 3. to throw into disorder.

These six areas were used in almost all the countries that were taken over by socialists and communists to change those countries' belief system. 1. Religion 2. Education 3. Social Life 4. Power Structure 5. Law & Order, and 6. Labor Relations

When the Russians changed their government to communism, they only spent 15% of their money, time, and manpower on espionage. The rest of the 85% was done through subversion.

This tactic was used first 2500 years ago by the Chinese adviser of the court Sun Rzu. He said the best way to fight is not war, but subvert (destroy the thinking).

Demoralization takes about 15-20 years to accomplish. That is the amount of time they say it takes to change the thinking of just one generation. They do this by teaching our children in public schools the socialist ideology. Once they have been indoctrinated with those ideas, it is almost impossible to change their way of thinking even if you give them countless information showing what they think is wrong.

They also take advantage of a group of people who are going against society's rules of government, religion, morals, freedoms, etc. and then they help push that group toward their ideals until the end result is that they have them hook, line, and sinker. They actually make the people think they are getting what they want, but the result will be a complete takeover.

Sound like today?

Our government is telling people, "We will take care of your healthcare, YOU DESERVE IT. We will make sure you are safe by taking guns off the streets, YOU DESERVE IT. We will make sure you make the same amount of money as your neighbor no matter how hard you work, YOU DESERVE IT. We will make sure you have the right to marry the same sex and not be spoken against it, YOU DESERVE IT."

It all sounds good on the surface, but later, I will reveal what is really taking place. Some of these statements will be repeated over and over, but you MUST GET THIS IN YOUR MINDS!!!!! THIS IS A PLAN TO OVERTHROW WHAT OUR COUNTRY IS AND IS FOUNDED ON!!!

Demoralization through Religion

To start to demoralize a nation, you must first dismantle its religion.

Religion is by far the most powerful thing on Earth. As you can see with ISIS, Christians, the Jews, and other faiths, people will die for their religion. That is why they attack religion first. What a person believes and has faith in, most of the time, is worth dying for.

This is why the communists try to destroy religion first. They openly admitted it in a Great Britain Socialist Party pamphlet, "Socialism and Religion," by stating, "It is therefore a profound truth that socialism is the natural enemy of religion. A Christian socialist is in fact an anti-socialist. Christianity is the antithesis of socialism."

For some of you who might not have a religion you have faith in, let's use a good long-time friend as an example. Let's say you have known this person all of your life. Ever since you have known them, they have always been the best person a community could ask for. They may have given millions of dollars to charity and personally helped people in need. They may have never gotten drunk, smoked, cursed, cheated on their spouse, or any other countless evil deeds as far as you knew and saw.

Then let's say on the local news, you see your friend's picture and the story of how they have brutally killed and tortured people for the past twenty years.

I'm am sure your first thought would be utter disbelief. You would probably defend this person and say they must have the wrong person because the person you know could never have committed such actions against another individual.

They begin to put on the media proof of DNA and other things that led them to believe they had the right person for the crime, but in your heart, you still don't think it to be true. Although they have tons of evidence that is both circumstantial and factual, you still refuse to believe your friend is guilty of these crimes. In fact, you might be the only person that thinks they are not guilty.

An example of this is O. J. Simpson and the charge of him killing his ex-wife and her boyfriend. Although there was a lot of evidence to show he did it, still the court let the man go free, and many believed he didn't do it.

One of the most damaging pieces of evidence in O. J.'s defense was the bloody glove they found with blood all over it. The defense team had O. J. put the glove on. You could see in O. J.'s eyes that he was worried about putting it on since this could be just enough to find him guilty. But to his shock and the shock of those around...it didn't fit. The defense team jumped on that, and one of his dream team attorneys, Johnny Cochran, made this famous statement, "If it doesn't fit, you must acquit."

I couldn't believe the prosecution didn't destroy that idea. Anyone knows that if a leather glove gets wet with blood and dries, it is going to shrink!!! But because of the faith in O. J. and his defense, O. J. was not charged for that crime.

This is a perfect example of how faith in a someone can make a person overlook key facts and turn it around to benefit their own position on what they believe.

When it comes to personal faith in a person's religion, that faith is even stronger. This is mostly because they themselves have experienced things that they feel could only have come about because of the faith they had in their religion.

When you add that this person's family may have had the same faith-based system, that further binds their firm conviction in their faith, making it almost impossible for anyone else to sway them from what they believe. These people, most of the time, as well as myself, are willing to die for what they believe in.

This is the reason they have to destroy a person's faith. If they don't do that, then the people will only fight and resist any attempt to take their faith and their ways of life from them. Once they dismantle a people's religion, the rest of subversion becomes so much easier.

So how do they destroy a person's religious belief?

First, they ridicule and make fun of religion. They try to make people believe they are stupid to believe in God, heaven, or hell. They make statements to make a believer look weak because the believer uses his faith as a crutch to make it in life. They have gone as far today as trying to label Christianity as a hate group and a terrorist organization.

It is obvious that they have never studied the Bible or understand what Christianity believes and teaches. The truth is, they are not concerned with truth. Their goal is to deceive and turn people against organized religion.

Once they have done that, the people will demand that Christians and others with high moral values be locked up or killed because they will believe the lie that such people are against others and causing trouble in the land. They believe these people are "intolerant" and label them as bigots.

As a side note, did you know that almost all of our pristine collages used to be Christian-based? That's right! Harvard and Yale were started by the Puritans. Princeton was started by Presbyterian believers. Princeton even today still has the motto, "Dei sub numine viget," Which is Latin for "Under God she flourishes." That sadly, even though posted as their motto is certainly not what is taught.

Oxford's founders were from different religious organizations, and Cambridge also was established by Christian leaders. So what caused these colleges to turn their backs on their foundation? Well, it surprisingly was because of Christians themselves.

What happened was, when man began to try and rationalize the Bible because of things he didn't understand, he found himself trying to find a reason. There are things in this world that we cannot explain. How did God create the Earth? How could it just take six days to do so? How was mankind able to understand with no teacher at first? Where do we go when we die?

These and countless other things can't be explained. In Christianity, it is all based on Faith, simple believing. If we are to believe the Bible, we must believe it ALL, not just what we can figure out that is logical.

When Christians began to try and explain things in a way they could understand, like evolution instead of creation, then it wasn't long before the rest of the Christian foundation began to fall apart.

While I am at it here, and it may be said later, if God says something is wrong, it's wrong! We can't say some parts of God's Word are true and that other parts are not. God's standard was, and should always be the standard that we put ourselves under.

Why am I talking about the Bible and God so much instead of other groups? Because this nation was first founded on Biblical principles and also with the freedom of religion. Our constitution and form of government were all set up under those beliefs.

From the very start, God played a significant role in forming our government. It was because of the desire to have the freedom to worship God that the founding fathers set off to find a place to do so, thus, the beginning of America.

America has since drifted far from this foundation. We, according to President Barak Obama, are no longer a Christian nation. I personally do not believe that President Obama was speaking for the majority of the American people. I believe that the majority, although not practicing what the Bible teaches, still believe that God and the Christian faith is an essential part of their lives. But because of the way our government is trying to dismantle our faith by many tactics, people don't speak out.

I personal desire to see that bold belief in God change back to the way our founding father's viewed America as was stated by George Washington in his first inaugural address, "No people can be bound to acknowledge and adore the invisible hand which conducts the affairs of men, more than the people of the United States."

These same people, when they set sail to find a country to worship God, did so on the prayer they prayed to God saying that if He blessed them on their journey, they promised to build a nation on His principles and evangelize the Christian faith.

Even though history is trying to be rewritten to remove God and the Christian faith from our foundation, there is still a witness to this truth by a picture that is in our nations rotunda showing the founding fathers and American people with knees bent and the Bible open. Don't be surprised if this isn't taken down in the next few years!

Then the movie industry started poking fun at religion with people like Flip Wilson and his famous line, "The devil made me do it." This made the devil appear to be a scapegoat for a person when they decide to do wrong. Just go ahead and do what you want, and when you get caught, blame the devil.

Although I myself believe that the devil can try to persuade you to do evil, the choice is and always will be YOUR decision. We are now a nation of people that take on no responsibility for their actions. They blame society, not being able to find a job, their upbringing, or a countless list of other excuses to blame for something they did.

I guess long gone are the days of honesty and personal responsibility as in the story of Abraham Lincoln, who ran miles down the road to give a customer back the correct change.

Then on to movies making fun of how preachers preach, making them look like dumb, redneck idiots. Now comedians and talk show hosts make blatant blasphemous statements without the fear of God's judgment.

The purpose of doing this is to get people to look upon people of faith as weirdos. It is also to make the people of faith feel cast away from the general population and the general ideas. It is to make them question their faith and belief system. It is to make them ashamed to voice how they believe.

Then they replace religion with FAKE religion like we see today. Preachers that never preach on sin, the blood, the need for salvation, the need to strive to live holy. They teach God is good and loves you without you having to do anything.

They never tell that the punishment of sin is death, but God has made a way of forgiveness. They preach how blessed you will be, but if you read the Word of God for yourself, God warns you will have hard times in this life, AND IT WILL GET WORSE, but He will be on your side and give you the strength to carry on.

They try and replace religion with sex cults and more to erode the basic foundation of religion and try to pull people away from the truths of God with the statement again, "IT'S YOUR RIGHT."

They have, in the past, used preachers of minority by playing on the minority's problems and woes. They make them believe they are genuinely concerned about those issues and want to help. They then program the pastors' minds with their propaganda and have them deliver that message to the congregations. We will discuss later how this then turns to civil unrest and violence.

Herbert W. Armstrong warned the Nation that both fascism and communism presented a threat to the American way of life. Just as he warned that a fascist revival of the old Holy Roman Empire would invade America if it turned away from God, he also warned that America's rejection of God would allow communism to weaken the country to where it could be invaded!

To further prove that the communist plan to destroy America includes getting rid of its religion, all you have to do is read this quote made by Joseph Stalin, "America is like a healthy body, and its resistance is threefold: its patriotism, its morality, and its spiritual life. If we can undermine these three areas, America will collapse from within."

Let me, for a moment, go back to the beginning when we were given our freedom of religion in this country. The protection of our freedom of religion was written in our First Amendment which states, "Congress shall make no law respecting an establishment of religion, or prohibiting the free exercise thereof; or abridging the freedom of speech, or of the press, or the right of the people peaceably to assemble and to petition the government for a redress of grievances." I don't know about you, but it appears to me that this was written to protect us from the government controlling our religious freedoms and right.

To me, our government for the last 20 years has crossed its line and has gone against the First Amendment on many occasions and circumstances. For instance, I recall just a few years before this book was written, a couple who owned a bakery refused to make a cake for a gay couple who were getting married because their religion didn't accept that type of behavior. The wedding couple sued the baking company and won in court. The couple who owned the bakery was told to either make the cake, or their business would be shut down.

Now it is none of my business what goes on behind close doors, but if my religion is against a behavior or action, I should have the right to stay by my convictions and refuse to offer any service that goes against what I believe. I am sure that there were several bakeries that would be more than willing to meet the need of that gay couple, but they wanted to make sure the one that didn't agree with their behavior would make the cake.

I wonder, say, if an atheist refused to provide a service for a church which might have said something against how the atheist believed, would they too be forced to provide the service the church asked for? It seems that Christianity is the only religion that has to be tolerant of others' actions.

The left has also gone against Chick-fil-a restaurant just because the founder doesn't believe in same-sex relationships. Although the restaurant chain has not refused to hire or serve any person that is in a same-sex relationship, nor do they advertise or promote what they believe about a same-sex relationship, they are still being attacked. When has it ever been ok for the government or the court system to come against a person's personal belief if they are not doing anything to others that causes the others harm?

Laws are being passed that come against preaching on gays. They have removed the ten commandments out of government buildings. They are trying to label religion as hate and terrorist groups, as I have mentioned before. They are not allowing us to preach on the streets anymore. They are trying to limit or stop altogether people who want to have Bible studies in their own homes. These are all actions to ban true religion in America and must be stopped now before they do so.

Demoralization through Education

Then they enter the education system. They teach to go green, the need to protect mother earth regardless of the cost, and that animals should be greater cared for more than humans.

Then the right to YOUR sexuality without the thought of God's concept. They tell people they should be proud of their sexuality and not let anyone say it is wrong. They fail to say to them that many times their bodies will suffer because of the lifestyle they choose because of things like aids.

They teach against creation and fill students' minds with evolution. They are teaching that we are no more than the monkeys, that we have just evolved to a higher position. They don't reveal to them, however, that even Darwin, who started that belief system, said he made it up and that he really didn't believe it but rather at the end of his life, trusted the Bible.

They begin to rewrite history so there will not be a trail of the past concerning the principles our nation was founded upon and has lived by.. They will make our founding fathers look like they were evil and power-hungry people. They do this to form the next generation to accept the new views and values in America.

Demoralization through Social Life

Next, they try and destroy social life. They do this by replacing individual places like churches with FAKE Bureaucratic bodies. Schools, arts, and entertainment are all geared to take away the values held by homes and churches.

Instead of social neighbors and friends, it changes to establish social worker institutions. It pushes away from close-knit neighbors and family for the good of ALL people instead of individual rights and needs.

Just for the record, all the praise you are hearing about how our government is passing laws they call "FOR THE GOOD OF THE PEOPLE," and stating that most America supports them, i.e., gay marriage, it is based on a one-sided poll put conducted by liberal media. They will only show the people who support these things, and if they show the opposite side, they will try to make them look like haters and crazy rednecks—just saying. Be wiser than that.

Demoralization through the Power Structure

Next, they hit the power structure. This is where normally a person would be elected by the people. They substitute it with people who were never elected to make the laws.

Our Supreme Court judges were not elected by the people but by the government. If the government is lawless, then the judges they appoint will also be, which in return will go against what most people with any sense of morality or judgment want.

We now have what is called the super delegates. They determine who will run for president. Even in our states, counties, and towns people who lobby make a lot of the rules instead of the ones who we have placed in office that are supposed to be listening to what we want to be passed. This all comes to one climax, taking the power structure. It keeps you from having your rights by the constitution.

Demoralization through Law & Order

Next, on the list is the demoralization of a nation, they attack law & order. They make the police look like they are power-hungry and abusive. They try and encourage sympathy for the criminal.

I am sure you can see this full-blown now with the past news events, "Cops shoot an unarmed black teen," "Cops use unnecessary force," "Suspect was mistreated."

This is where they pick a few corrupt cops, and some good cops, to try and make the people believe you can't trust them.

They try to make the criminal look like the victim. They show pictures of the teens when they were small and not the size of a linebacker when they come running at the officer. They fail to mention how the unarmed suspect was trying to get the officer's gun or was beating them, attempting to knock them out so they could get the officer's gun. They fail to mention how the suspect had a weapon but threw it in the crowd who took it and hid it from the police. I will give plenty of examples further in the book on cases like these that have happened.

Their goal is to cause mistrust in the people against local law enforcement. It's to create civil unrest. It's to divide the nation using religion, race, or anything that binds us together because they know "United we Stand, Divided we Fall." This opens the door for the government to come in and take control by martial law, so they say, "to protect the people."

Demoralization through Labor Relations

Finally, they attack labor relations. They change the normal labor relations between a company and worker where the company sets wages, and people decide if they want to work there or not and turn it into a government/worker relationship.

This is where the government mandates your pay amount, work conditions, and how everything is distributed. In other words, the government controls everything, the money, the workers, and the products and the government determines who and what gets some back.

What they push for is that everyone gets a paycheck from the government either by wages or hand-outs. Why? So, they can control how wealthy and powerful you become. Once they are in control, however, they will make sure that every person will work for pennies.

We have seen this for years with our give away programs. Now more than ever, we see hand-outs to illegals and people who don't want to work. People who never save to buy a home are given loans and money to get one.

Once again, this all sounds good on paper, but the end result is to have control over the people by making them dependent on the government for their survival.

One of the latest advances on this is the Supreme Court upholding the Obama-care program. government controlled insurance. Also, included were the bank bail-out; government banking and control of money, the auto bail-out, government private factory control.

All of the things mentioned above are pushed by propaganda, making people believe they are working for the people to promote equality, which in reality once again, it's about GOVERNMENT CONTROL.

While working on a project on 6/26/2015, I had a break-in news report on my phone stating the Supreme Court ruled in favor of gay marriages. This is just one more aspect of how the government takes control of our lives and freedoms of speech, religion, and the constitution that was created to protect us from government power.

Because of this passing, I can no longer marry anyone because if I am a preacher, and refuse to marry a gay couple because of my personal religious beliefs that it goes against God's laws, I will be fined or put in prison. Soon if not already included in the law, I won't even be able to mention what God says about that lifestyle.

ARE YOU GETTING THE PICTURE HERE?!! THE PURPOSE IS FOR GOVERNMENT CONTROL!!!! IT'S PAST TIME TO WAKE UP AMERICA!!!!

The Bible does support equality, but only as it demands each person to take responsibility for his/her actions and do what is necessary to achieve their own goals by working with their own hands. But if a country turns its back on God, the nation will pay the price!!!

You may feel that what our government is doing is for the good of the people. But as in Russia, when they finally get full control, if you are born with a disability where you can't work, or you get old, or something happens in your life where you can't work, they will kill you because you have become a burden to the GOOD OF SOCIETY.

You will be fined, punished, imprisoned, tortured, or killed for speaking your beliefs because it will be considered a threat to the GOOD OF SOCIETY. This already has a path to be enforced through our so-called Patriot Act. We will be labeled terrorists if we are a believer in the Bible because of the stance the Bible makes on certain things.

Never is it good for anyone to have full power. With absolute power comes absolute corruption. There are many case studies that prove this!!!!

Man, by nature, is not concerned about others. Man left to himself will kill everything in his path to get on top.

Only with God as our leader will we ever become a moral, secure, and powerful nation. Pray for a revival in America!! It may be too late already.

To find out more about the author go to:
www.treeoflifecoaching.org

Chapter 5

Phase II -- Crisis

Once these steps are completed comes the next area which is crisis.

Besides the attacking of our Christian faith and beliefs and our southern heritage, gag orders, pushing race issues, making the police look like the enemy, and so forth, this make people turn on one another.

It's already happening. The Black Panthers now have vowed to FINISH what they started by killing all the whites, and the KKK is rising up again as well. The gays are fighting hard against the church, and the church is trying to keep its freedom. They use natural disasters and diseases as well to cause a crisis.

This brings about an out of control mass of people causing crisis throughout the nation. In return, this gives the government the right to step in and call for martial law, the exercise of government control by military authorities over the civilian population of a designated territory.

Chapter 6

Phase – III Normalization

Once the unrest of the people is so great that martial law is implemented, then the government sets all standards of which is the final process they will call normalization.

This, in short, means whatever the government says is right you will do, and if you don't, you will be locked away or killed. You will believe it is the norm.

People, let me warn you, once the crisis process starts, it usually just takes 2-6 months before the government takes full control!!!! We are well past that, and better be prepared for a major change!!!

All the chaos you are seeing on the local news is not what it seems. The underlying movement is communism. The communists infiltrate these movements to help stir it toward their goal.

Even the great speech by Dr. Marin Luther King, Jr., "I have a dream," was able to be delivered by people who made like they were a part of that movement. But, the very one that organized the event so that Dr. Maring Luther King, Jr, could deliver that speech was a communist.

The main goal in this normalization process is to make anything immoral, unjust, anti-government, and anti-capitalist all appear normal and accepted. Anyone that stands for values and morality will be silenced. We can see how all this comes into play later on in the book.

Chapter 7

Phase – IV DESTABILIZATION

We talked about the first process of taking over a nation was through subversion and the steps to make it happen.

After a group of people who are trying to overthrow a nation through subversion has accomplished the demoralization of the country, they will try to destabilize it, which generally takes 2-5 years to do.

Remember, it takes 15-20 years to demoralize a country because it takes that long to corrupt the minds of one generation. I thought it essential to bring out here, we are now on our 3rd generation of corrupted thinking through demoralization in this country.

Shocking isn't it? Because of this, it will make it three times harder to try to turn the country back around, without supernatural intervention, because we will have to train up at least two newer generations to counter what has already been put in the minds of the ones under the demoralization process.

There are fewer steps needed to destabilization because the major groundwork has now been completed, and you have a generation that is behind this new order.

To destabilize you need the following steps:
Step one is Power struggle. We have seen this big time in the past ten years of our government.

There is a new push toward populistic ideals. This mainly deals with taking from the rich and giving to the poor, in essence. History has proven itself time and time again that it just doesn't work.

There are now so many people in America who feel they are "ENTITLED," maybe because they live in a poor area, or, because of their ancestry, think they are limited in being able to make it big. Whatever the reason, these are just excuses for them to get FREE MONEY OR HELP.

In order to accomplish destabilization, you have to have almost complete government control of all things. Money, businesses, religion, and personal rights all fall under this category. Thus BIG BROTHER is set up to make sure all people follow the rules.

In the past two elections, we had one party saying we need less government and less government spending, and even maybe less taxes. The other side was saying we need more government control "FOR THE GOOD OF THE PEOPLE."

It only takes common sense to figure out which one is right. You can't keep giving away more and more money and not have people pay their part. Sooner or later, you will run out of money, and whomever you borrowed it from will collect whatever you own to get their investment back.

America never was established for FREE STUFF. It was founded on OPPORTUNITY. If you work hard for it, you can do whatever you want.

The Bible backs this kind of thinking as well. Genesis 3:19 (KJV) "In the sweat of thy face shalt thou eat bread, till thou return unto the ground; for out of it wast thou taken: for dust thou art, and unto dust shalt thou return."   In other words, if you want something, WORK FOR IT!!!

We could go on and on here on the different ideas but the main thing I want to warn you of when you hear your politicians speak is this, if they are saying things like, "tax the rich to help the poor"; "we are looking out for the good of everyone so that all can be equal", the word "equality", "new government", and so on... RUN FROM THAT PERSON!!! Their main goal is for total government control.

Step 2 is economy. You will see that almost all of these points now work hand and hand.

In the economy, they will try to control how businesses do business. They are working now to make people pay time and half for anything over 40 hours in companies that have so-called manager positions or whatever and are on a salary. Once again, sounds good, but the reason for the involvement is government control.

Everyone has the right to work where they want. If you don't like your job, if you feel you aren't getting paid enough, FIND ANOTHER JOB; but don't allow the government to tell a business what they can and can't do. It is the freedom of commerce that keeps a country striving for better.

How so? Competition!!! If you don't give the best product and wages for your employees to help get your product out, your business will fail.

Once the government gets involved, businesses have so much on their heads trying to please the "entitled-minded people" they must close. Thus, the Government has to step in and give away more money, which, in return, causes the country to go bankrupt, and then full government control must take over.

They also try and control how the business is run like they tried to do with Hobby Lobby and the healthcare system, telling Hobby Lobby they must obey the healthcare law even though it went against Hobby Lobby's religious belief.

They also are trying to do that now with the poor couple that had the bakery even going as far as to put a gag order on the couple not allowing them to tell citizens of the United States that the government has closed their business and sued them for over $130,000 because they wouldn't bake a cake for a gay couples' wedding. They refused because they were Christians and didn't believe in gay marriages.

As a side note, Greece just recently lost all of its money, and the direct cause was from all the giveaway programs the government had. Canada and Puerto Rica are following close behind facing the same gloom. GIVEAWAYS JUST DON'T WORK!!!

But understand this, our government knows it doesn't work. It is all in the plan to make money fail, so your hard-earned dollars are worthless, and they can make a new system of money and laws that they will control.

Step 3 is social fiber, law

This is where our basic fundamental beliefs are being taken away and replaced with newer ideas. You can understand this with everything that has happened just this past year at a fever pitch.

They removed the confederate flag. They are removing the ten commandments. A church is being sued by the LGBT to force their agenda. The Supreme Court is making laws which is the job of Congress, not a body that wasn't elected by its people to pass laws.

Anything that has to do with morality, Godly, or patriotic value is being attacked as old-school thinking. They are now even going to teach our small children that are not in high school yet about oral and anal sex, homosexuality and transgenderism, all motivated to push the idea on these children that it is ok to do and normal. Yet it is forbidden to teach about God's laws and standards.

Finally, the last step is 4. Foreign relations. The way we handle business with foreign nations.

I won't even go into all the deals made secretly with other countries because of our government's fear of them. We are working on trying and to form a nation with rules run by the United Nations.

When that happens, we will be forced to go by the United Nation's rules over what our constitution says. This again will give our government full control over its people.

We, as the United States of America, should always stand for our individuality and freedom above all else. That is what has made America great in the past and will keep her great in the future.

Chapter 8

2020

As I begin writing this chapter in the year 2020, I am amazed that I am now in my 60's! I was born in 1958, and it just seems like yesterday that I was playing with the neighborhood kids after school. The years seem to have flown by so quickly.

During my 60 plus years, I have seen so many changes in America. When I was a young boy, we only had three television stations in the metro Atlanta area, and all were black and white.

There was only one television in the home, and it was a 19-inch floor model. I was never allowed to decide what we were going to watch because dad had full control of that. We did have a remote though; it was ME!!!

There was no high definition. It was fuzzy most of the time. All we had was what was called a rabbit ear antenna on the top of the television. We would put aluminum foil on the top of the metal rods to try and get a better signal, and all of the stations went off the air at midnight.

In December of 1976, Ted Turner started channel 17, TBS, which was a UHF channel. Soon after, channel 30, 36 and 46 were added. We were in the big leagues now!

We lived in a tiny two-bedroom brick home. Dad added another bedroom and den later on. But behind our street of small houses, a contractor came in and built split-level homes that were around 1,800 square feet in size. The only ones that could afford houses that nice were people who had high-paying jobs like airplane pilots. We were impressed.

Most families in those days had one car, and most women stayed home. We had two vehicles, and mom worked. We didn't have much, but it was home, and we were content.

Our lifestyle consisted of mom and dad working Monday-Friday, while I went to school. On the weekend, mom would go to the grocery store. Every Sunday we would be at church during the morning and evening service.

Our vacation was usually once a year when we would go see our family in Virginia. I didn't even see the beach until I was 14 years old, and the only reason for that was because I went on vacation with my older sister one year.

We had one landline telephone. If you were away from home, you just missed whoever may have been calling, no matter if it were an emergency or not. We were later blessed to get an answering machine, but we felt we had it much better than our kinfolk in the mountains. They had what was called a party line. With that, about five families would be connected to a service. So if you wanted to make a call and your neighbor was on the phone, you could hear them talking and had to wait till they hung up.

There were no cell phones, google maps, or computers. If you wanted to go on a trip, you would buy a paper map of every city you planned on going to so you would know how to get there. And if you were traveling on Sunday, you hoped that not all of the gas stations would be closed for the day.

I was young enough to remember when de-segregation first started in the school system. I watch as the first man stepped foot on the moon. I watched in horror as Dr. Marin Luther King Jr. and many others were beaten for trying to cross a bridge in Selma, Alabama, and also the shocking news of President Kennedy being shot and killed. I still remember his casket on the train and also going down the road pulled by a horse.

I have seen society change from being able to sleep at night without locking the doors to being fearful ever to do such a thing. I've watched the hippy movement, drugs filling our schools, and police having to walk our hallways in the school.

I remember people building fallout shelters during the cold war with Russia. I remember America going in and out of battles. I remember our brave soldiers who fought in Vietnam coming home only to be ridiculed and shamed by people.

Yes, I have seen many changes in my lifetime, but nothing like I have seen in the past 15 years, and especially after Trump was elected and the year 2020. I, for the first time in my life, am now fearful of where our nation is heading.

2020 not only stands for a year in time, but when you place a forward slash between the 20's it becomes 20/20, which is considered perfect vision. I believe that we now have a 20/20 view of where our government is trying to lead American, and it is not pretty.

If you were to tell me 15 years ago that our nation would be where it is today, I would have said you must be out of your mind. Never in a million years would I have dreamed that peoples' views of America, its history, its flag, and its constitution would be under such an attack.

Never would I have believed that there would be such disrespect to our police officers, or for that matter, our elderly. But this didn't happen overnight, and it wasn't a surprise to some.

In 1958, the very year I was born, a former FBI employee by the name of W. Cleon Skousen wrote a book entitled "The Naked Communist." This book goes into great detail about the communist party.

We have already discussed what the former KGB leader Yuri Bezmenov warned us about, how communists take over a country. Now I want to turn our attention to another starch warning that was given in the past to America.

W. Cleon Skousen, book "The Naked Truth", was the source of the publication of the "1963 Communist Goal" that Skousen entered into the Congressional Record.   It list of 45 goals of the communist plan to overthrow our Country."

In this chapter, we will go over most of the list and show how most of these goals have been fulfilled in this nation just 60 years later! It may be too late to stop our nation from going communist, but we must try for the sake of our kids and grandkids.

The first item tells how the United States should coexist (to get along no matter the difference in ideas or opinions) with all other countries as the only alternative to atomic war.

I can agree with that one for the most part. Yes, we should all try to get along in this world. Even our Bible that most American's believe in, tells us to work and live peacefully with each other. Romans 12:18, "If it be possible, as much as lieth in you, live peaceably with all men". However, we should never compromise our values and beliefs to fit in.

In the next item, it said the United States should capitulate (given in, surrender) to, at that time, Russia to prevent atomic war. The Russians had caused the American people to be terrified that Russia would drop an Atomic bomb on us. So, in essence, to keep that from happening, according to the list of items to overthrow America, Americans should surrender ourselves to Russia if the option came to surrender or engage in war.

If you have noticed, it has been a long fight to cut spending on our military. Many of our leaders want to cut way back on our military power. They try to make it seem that it is a waste of money and that we are trying to flex our arms to the rest of the world.

As bad as it may sound, a strong military is a deterrent that actually makes other countries less likely to attack America because of her strong defense. I have always heard the statement, "The bigger they are, the harder they fall." However, what no one told me, was it usually is harder to make them fall in the first place. We must remember and never let it fail, that a strong military is our best defense of another country taking us over.

Item 3 in the list ties in with the second but tries to convince America to disarm herself to show the world how much moral value we have toward humans and how we want to get along with everyone. There is a movement in America today that still is trying to make Americans believe that we appear to be bullies to the world because of our military power. However, they don't complain about Russia, China, or any other country that has just as much military force as the U. S.

I can completely understand why the world would want to disarm a country that has a dictator who appears to have no concern for human rights and seems to have a desire to take over the World or mistreat their own people. However, America has a check and balance before we can use our most potent weapons, which gives an added measure of safety to help prevent someone from acting irresponsibly or out of fear.

We shouldn't allow others to make us feel like we should be ashamed of our power. It is because of America's strength that other dictators have been conquered, thus freeing that country's citizens.

It is not immoral to have a nation with a massive military to defend itself. It instead, is vital that America stays on top of the list of powerful Nations so other countries will most likely not do harm to its people or attack smaller countries, with the fear that America's wrath will come upon them.

Think of what would have happened to the Jews had not America been a part of the resistance to overtake Hitler. Think of what would have happened to thousands more women and children had America not put an end to Saddam Hussein. Not to mention how much more America would suffer at the hands of terrorism had not our power and intelligence stopped Osama bin Laden. And that is just a few examples of why we need our robust defense system.

The list included allowing free trade between all countries with no limits, no matter if the country is a communist nation or not, no matter if the items sent could be used against us or another country such as items to make weapons or biological warfare, no matter if the country had a dictator that was torturing its people.

It seems every time that one of our leaders tries to stop free trade with a country that is hurting others or has a communistic view, we have demonstrators bulking against it and trying to make us look like we are the problem, not the country committing the crimes.

I sometimes wonder if the protestors are that ignorant, or are they being paid by someone to protest and are doing it for the money. Surely to God, if a person who cares at all about humanity, he wouldn't protest cutting off supplies to someone whos aim is to harm others!

It should be one of our utmost concerns not to support anyone or a country that is out to harm others. Imagine how you would feel if you knew that America was helping a nation that your family lives in, where the leader of that country is raping the women and killing the kids. How would you feel? Would free trade with no holds barred sound like a good idea to you? I think not!

Oh, and don't kid yourself. I believe there are countries that we usually wouldn't help or support, that we do help for our own selfish gain to get something from them that we may need. Eventually, that country will come back and bite the hand that feeds them.

The communist plan also included giving long-term loans to not only Russia but the Soviet satellites. That would be the same as an intruder coming inside your home and you handing them a gun. Not a good idea! Common sense would tell a person not to aid in helping an enemy gain power or intelligence that could be used against them.

They also want the United States to give aid to all countries as they do with free trade, with no boundaries even if the country is communist and hurting their own people.

I would say that America is one of the biggest givers when it comes to aid. We give countless millions to other countries, yet when America is in need, how much of that comes back our way. Practically none!!!

We not only give aid in money, but we have in the recent past, given some of our most sophisticated weapons to our sworn enemies! Why would one of our leaders ever do such a thing! The only answer I can come up with is either greed or to help the cause to bring our nation to a communist structure.

As a side note, it was in our government's budget to give over $52 billion in aid during the 2020 year. That seems like a whole lot of money, considering that we can't even pay the interest on the money we have borrowed from other countries combined with how little we give to our veterans and elderly. I feel we should take care of our own first before handing out to others.

We rarely do a check on what the countries are doing with the aid we send. It has been proven that hundreds of millions of people were annihilated or tortured as a direct result of the assistance given. This shows that many times the aid given to people in charge trying to control the people instead of to the people who need the assistance.

There are many countries that genuinely need and depend on our aid, and we should continue to supply them with it. However, we should be good stewards with the money that "the people" of the United States gave, to make sure it is spent wisely and that it is not used to further a dictator or corrupt government. When given to those types of leaders, the people usually are left hungry, poor, and weak.

This may come as a shock to you as well. The top two countries we give aid to are countries that support terrorism and want to destroy the United States. They are Afghanistan at $4.89 billion and Iraq at $3.36 billion. I wonder just how much of that money has been used to cause trouble in our own nation?

Just in passing, one of the things on the list was to recognize Red China and admit them to the U. N., which happened during the presidency of Jimmy Carter. Also, in the past, they wanted to prolong conferences dealing with the ban of atomic testing because America had agreed that it would suspend the testing as long as the negotiations were going on. This they did.

One of the big items in this list that made me quiver at my spine was they wanted to have the U. N. as the ONLY hope for mankind!!! They also put in the list that if its charter were rewritten, they would demand it be set up as a one-world government with its own independent armed forces.

This upset me in many ways. One of which deals with what the Bible talks about when dealing with a one-world government. I will discuss that later in this book.

A one-world government has been the desire of many people in the past. Napoleon, Hitler, Stalin, and many others wanted a one-world government. Surprisingly, many of our government leaders are trying their best to make it happen as well.

Did you notice that in this system, they wanted their own armed forces? Do you think this just might have anything to do with the current situation in the year 2020 of people trying to get rid of the police and our military? I believe I can prove it has a direct tie later in the book as well when we go over some of the radical groups protesting today.

I think it also should be noted who started the U. N. in the beginning. It was started by communist leaders themselves, such as Alger Hiss who was an American government official. He was accused of spying for the Soviet Union in 1948, but they found out too late to make any charges of espionage to stick. He was later charged with a much less offense. Talk about sleeping with the enemy!

Item 12 in the list says to resist any attempt to outlaw the communist party. You would think America would fight hard against communism, but the fact is, we have embraced it with open arms.

When I was young, I was so fearful that the communists would invade and take over America. We knew the truth of what communism would bring when it took over a country. If a person even hinted that they were for communism, they were under a watchful eye from then on.

But today, the goals they set back in 1963 have already weakened the government's ability to investigate any type of subversion in this country. As a matter of fact, by them being able to accomplish item 15 in the list, they now have a stronghold on America and are passing laws to further their agenda.

So, what is in item 15? Their goal was to take over one or both of the political parties of America. Can you guess which one they were able to take over?

This political communist-driven party didn't happen in just the past few years. It is just reaching the point where that party has such a supporting force, that they are no longer fearful of being discovered for who they really are.

In this 2020 election, it seems almost like déjà vu of 1979. It was during the presidential election that a man named Peter Schweizer wrote a book entitled "Regan's War" in which he exposed just how much the communist party and their supporters had infiltrated that particular political party in our country. That was back in 1979. Imagine how much more they have a hold now! I strongly suggest you get a copy of this book and see just how much we have gravitated toward embracing the communist ideology.

How could America allow this party to continue to get a stronghold over America? It's simple; you just keep promising that you will give things the people want and they will vote you into position.

They promise free health care, free school, bailouts to help if your business fails, free housing, and the list goes on.

The problem is, they will never do what they promised, nor can they. There is no way that we, as a nation, can provide all this. It would bankrupt the country. It doesn't take a financial wizard to understand that you can't borrow your way to success.

The sad thing is most of the people who vote for that particular party, believe they are going to get all that is promised and that it will help them climb the ladder in economics. They genuinely believe that the party cares about their status in society and is trying to help them out. But the fact is, it only further keeps them in bondage by allowing the government to have full control of their lives.

Another of the goals is to do away with any kind of loyalty oaths. This one is almost funny if it wasn't so sad. Most of the people who take an oath to defend our nation are liars and have no desire to keep America secure and hold fast to the values and principles it was founded upon.

Integrity seems to be a word that has been forgotten in America. Integrity is doing the right thing even when no one is looking. Instead, we have hundreds of our government leaders taking bribes and making deals with the enemy to further their careers or fatten their wallets. THEY ARE SELLING OUT OUR COUNTRY!!!!

In item 14, they want Russia to continue to have access to our Patent Office. This may not sound all that alarming, but when you understand that opens the door to all of our information on developing weapons, vaccines, and technology, it can be a dangerous thing.

Items 16 through 42 look more like watching our current morning news. People, we better wake up and wake up fast. Remember, these are goals they were trying to accomplish in 1963. If they didn't do anything until now, they have made drastic headway in the past four years to get these accomplished.

Because these are now current events, I will mesh all these together so you can see for yourself what is going on in America. Some items have been discussed already. Some will be discussed in more detail later on. I feel it necessary to repeat over and over what is going on, so it will embed in our minds the reality of what is around us.

As most of us watch the evening news, we are troubled in our spirits when we see the chaos and hatred that fills the news. How did we get to this point? Where did all these haters of America come from? Why isn't our government doing something to stop the madness?

It's not that it hasn't been happening all along. It's that we have quietly sat back and let it happen ever so slowly. We've been conditioned to believe a lie. We are sympathetic to causes that seem to be good in theory but have a hidden agenda. Let's look at the list of goals and see how it has happened.

One of the groups that have been very influential in destroying American values and ushering in this socialistic movement is the American Civil Liberties Union and the NAACP. Many of the leaders of those organizations are communists. They get involved in any social issue they can and twist it to cause division and chaos.

Their primary focus is to use the court system to pass laws to weaken institutions and organizations by stating their activities or principles are violating the civil rights of others. News Flash!!! No institution or organization can do anything without it offending or stepping on someone else's rights or beliefs. We all have different ideas and goals. If you don't like what an organization or institute believes in, go to another or start your own. In America, you are free to do that!

In the list of goals, the communists wanted to control the schools and the schools' papers. By doing so, they could start at an early age of a child to indoctrinate them into the communist and socialist ideology. They fill the school with communist propaganda that teaches them that socialism is a way for people to be equal and that capitalism is a way to make the rich richer and the poor weaker.

They fill our school system with people who are a part of, or sympathetic to, the advancement of communism. These people also create the curriculum that the school will abide by.

They reject free-thinking and teach things like global warming, protecting the environment, and equality for all. They teach that fundamental religion is wrong and dangerous.

Once these students are brainwashed into thinking socialism is good for America, you cannot change their minds even if you have a whole building with proof showing it isn't.

After they have convinced the students that the old ways of America were a form of social injustice, the students are then used to riot and protest to stop what the students think is "injustice." In reality, however, they are helping the communist party take over. Have you noticed who the majority of the ones causing the riots and protest in our nation today are? Yep, young people.

The school system is essential because it forms a whole generation to believe in a particular thought. It is one of the most powerful tools that the Communist uses.

Young people are vulnerable and easy to deceive. They have little experience of life. They haven't lived long enough to see the long-term effects of bad decisions. That is why it is so imperative for parents to spend time teaching their children the truth and warning them of what they hear in classrooms and from peers.

The next primary tool that is used and is very active today is the media. Their goal to infiltrate and control critical positions in the media and movie industry has been accomplished. You might not agree when you have heard President Trump call the news "Fake News," but the fact is, almost all news media outlets are owned by the progressive socialist party or are in line with that kind of thinking.

The control of news, newspapers, books, movies, and the like will dictate what people believe to be true. It works like gossip. If you only hear one side of the story, you will believe that side. The news was supposed to be completely unbiased, but as you see every night on your local news station, it isn't!

To many people, some of our actors in the movies are their heroes. They are their role models. Unfortunately, those that live in Tinsel Town have no idea of what is going on in the real world, and many of them embrace communism and socialism.

Many of the actors are also anti-American and against American values. People like Whoopi Goldberg, Rosie O'Donnell and others making fun of our president and his family. People like Robert DeNiro disrespecting the president and saying he wished he could punch him in the face. These statements show the hatred toward our American system and culture. It is ironic how their comments are allowed and embraced, but anything that stands strong for American culture is silenced, ridiculed, and if you work for a company, you can be fired over. Our values are considered hate, racism, and intolerable.

The Communist goal is not only to discredit our American culture through the avenues mentioned above but also in art. Any art that stands for good is to be eliminated and replaced with artwork that has no meaning. They are quoted to say in Item 23, "Our plan is to promote ugliness, repulsive, meaningless art."

In items 24-26, they attack our morality. They want to eradicate all laws that govern obscenity. They say it is censorship, and it comes against our freedom of speech, expression, and free press.

They further this goal by breaking down our standards and morality. Pornography, homosexuality, and other forms of obscenity are used in our books, magazines, and movies. Even today, a child's doll was produced and sold in department stores that when you touch her private parts, it moans with pleasure. There are other dolls which, when you place their naked bodies in the water, fishnet and provocative clothing, along with "tramp stamps" would appear. Shocked?! You should be; it is happening right before our eyes.

Their goal here is to make homosexuality, sex outside of marriage, open relationships, friends with benefits, bestiality, pedophilia, and the like a normal, acceptable, and healthy way of life. Anyone that opposes is old-fashioned and is a bigot. They are shamed, silenced, and threatened to the point where the moral majority will stay quiet. I will show how easily this was accomplished through Antonio Gramsci and his plan to overthrow the Christian belief system in another chapter.

From here, it made it easier for the communists to move into the next two items, which dealt with religion. They are making significant advances as they have already infiltrated the Catholic seminaries, Conservative and Reformed Judaism, the Nation Council of Churches, and are hard at work to infiltrate every protestant religion.

Their work, once inside, is to change true religion into a social religion by discrediting some of our central valued Bible beliefs and even to make the Bible appear to be full of mistakes. They make statements that I am sure you have heard such as, "religion and belief in God is just a crutch to a weak-minded person." They don't want sound doctrine preached, but an easy belief and socially accepted program.

They used the "separation of church and state" to stop prayer in our schools, and now at games or sporting events. They are working hard, and to some degree, ended prayer as an opening to government forums. The purpose of "separation of church and state" was not for the government to control church behavior but rather to keep the government out of the church.

The next three items that were on the list of goals dealt with the breaking down of America's foundation, leaders, and history. Once again, this is a goal that we see coming to fruition every night on our local news station. Their goal was to discredit the constitution of America and its founding fathers, to put down our culture, and remove our history.

Every night, you can see in one state or another, people taking down statues of confederate leaders from the past. Here in Georgia, there is a big push to remove the carving on Stone Mountain because it is offensive to many because of the history it represents.

Not only the public but even our government leaders, including those in the White House, are actively trying to change our constitution. They call it outdated, or not for the good of the people today. Not only our constitution, but are bound and determined to do away with our Bill of Rights. All in the name for the good of the people mind you!

They are trying not only to remove our history but to rewrite it. The purpose is to twist the truth of our past and fashion it so it can be used to justify the changes they want to bring.

Instead of teaching more on our history and values and why it is essential and works, they are pushing their social agenda and deceiving the masses into believing they are missing out on something great.

One of the tactics use is to make someone feel bad if they have more than another person. They use shame and guilt if you somehow have worked hard to be successful and try to make you feel you should share your success with others less fortunate. "Privileged" is the new term used to try and shame people who have worked hard for what they have accumulated.

More of the items on the list are to support any socialist movement to gain control of the educational system, social agencies, mental health clinics, welfare programs, pharmaceutical companies, psychiatric professions, or any other program that has the power to have control over the people.

Items 33 and 34 are to stop any form of laws that block the communist movement as well as do away with the House Committee on Un-American Activities.

Items 36 and 37 are to gain more control of unions and big businesses.

Items 35 and 38 deal with taking power away from the FBI and the police force. Their goal is to give the power of correction to the mental institutes (that they control) claiming that only a trained psychologist can help a criminal change their behavior. This will eventually allow them to lock away and even torture anyone that gets in the way to stop the communist takeover or progress by classifying them as a terrorist or a traitor to the cause.

Item 40 has been fulfilled for years now. It was to dismantle the family institution. We now have more laws that help people that have been divorced than to help people trying to keep a family together. Over 50% of marriages now end in divorce. It is now socially accepted to be divorced or even have an extramarital affair.

They know that the family is one of the most substantial ties that can bind the communist from taking over. This can best be seen in families without a father figure. Most of the time, those children end up in a life of crime.

Item 41 states the need to raise children away from the negative influences of parents. It sounds like a good thing, doesn't it? The problem lies in their plan. As stated, many times in this book, the communist agenda has no concern with the individual but the control over that individual.

You see, with them having control of our children and what they are being taught, they now can take away a child simply because they are being taught that there is a God. Or God forbid, you teach principles in the Bible like homosexual behavior is not good.

Don't think they will not take them away. Over 30 years ago, I had a friend that DFAC took their children because they had a strong Christian belief and lived their life according to it. Shocking, isn't it?

Item 42 is another goal that we are now seeing in the news nightly. It states that violence and insurrection are legitimate aspects of getting what you want.

They first taught this to the young people to get them motivated to take such actions. What makes me upset the most, however, is that our politicians have bought into this lie or are behind it and encourage that terroristic behavior, even going as far as letting them do it without punishment or consequences.

Then to make matters worse, our good ole actors and sports leaders are paying the bond to set these low-lives free if they do get locked up. How twisted is that thinking? I had wondered if they would still think the same if it happened to them until I heard that Target, after being destroyed in a city, said it was ok that they destroyed and looted their store. They understood the hurt and pain.

HOGWASH! That is the problem with people in America now! We have no personal accountability for the actions one does to another, or another's property. Can you imagine what the next generation will be like if we don't stop this madness now?!

Listed below are items 43 through 44 just for your reference.

43. Overthrow all colonial governments before native populations are ready for self-government.

44. Internationalize the Panama Canal. Note: In 1999 we gave the power back to Panama.

And last but not least... Item 45. Repeal the Connally Reservation so the U.S. cannot prevent the World Court from seizing jurisdiction over domestic problems. Give the World Court jurisdiction over domestic problems. Give the World Court jurisdiction over nations and individuals alike.

So, what does that mean? It means that the laws and protections we have under the United States of America can be taken away at any given moment.

It means that the World Court can and will take away our police, FBI, CIA, and other law enforcement and replace them with the U.N. military if they deem necessary. It means the World Court can not only dictate what our country does but what each and every one of its citizens can do or believe.

Well, there you have it, the 1963 documented goals of the communist party for the United States of America. You also now know that our government leaders have been well aware of this all these years and obviously chose not to do anything about it but rather have helped it along.

ARE YOU WAKING UP YET!!! YOU BETTER BE BECAUSE THEY ARE COMING THROUGH OUR DOORS AT THIS VERY MOMENT!!!

In the next chapter, I want to discuss some of the movements and organizations that are so powerful in our nation and are going under the pretense of the betterment of our society.

Chapter 9

UNCOVERING THE CURRENT MOVEMENTS IN AMERICA!

There has, for as long as I can remember, been protests and organizations trying to change specific values or beliefs in America. Some have been good and some bad.

Sadly, the communist party has either infiltrated some of these movements, or their founders are communist ideologist. The communists are brilliant at stirring the pot and making it look like it is for the betterment of the people as I have said so many times in the book.

In this chapter, we are going to take a look at some of the past and present organizations and movements. We want to see the purpose of why they started and the founders of them. We will also look into whether they have a hidden agenda they don't want America to know.

The current movements of today, to me, have been the most devastating in America's history. As I go over some of them, you may feel that I am being biased or even prejudiced, but believe me, I am only trying to show what impact these movements will have on our freedom in the future.

I was told by one of my own immediate family whom I had loved, cared for, and even stood up for when I knew they were in the wrong, that I was more patriotic than I was caring because I wouldn't say Black Lives Matter only. They further told me what a disappointment I was to them.

Of course, that was a cut to the throat to me. However, they were right about one thing; I am very patriotic. If we ever lose our American freedom, NO LIFE WILL MATTER! It is far from the truth that I don't care about a particular race or person, but I know enough about communism and socialism to know that if we head that direction, all the people I love will suffer.

My goal in this book is not to try and sound insensitive but to warn about what is about to change that will end America as we know it if strong measures are not taken NOW! You can never get a group of people to agree on everything, and everyone has their right to their opinion. You can take my views or discard them as conspiracy, but if you discard them, be ready to face the consequences of you closing a blinded eye to what's going on.

So, with that in mind, let us take a look at the past to the present and see if we can find anything that might suggest we are on the wrong path.

The African American Civil Rights

I guess this movement is one of the dearests to me and is a treasure to my heart, probably because the effects were seen in my early childhood years. I was able to witness a lot of the success of this movement.

It is also known as the Civil rights movement and the Freedom Movement. The Civil Rights movement was gaining momentum in the '40s and '50s but, in my personal opinion, hit its main force in 1955 when Dr. Marin Luther King, Jr. took the reins to lead the organization in peaceful protest for not only the blacks, but whites and other peoples' equal rights as well.

Although the 14th and 15th amendments in 1868 and 1870 gave blacks equal protection and the right to vote, still, many southern states fought hard against it and refused to obey the laws passed. On the contrary, much of the south lived by what was known as the Jim Crow laws. Those laws didn't allow blacks the same rights to schools, jobs, or even the right to vote. This law was in effect from the post years of the Civil War all the way to 1968.

Many other issues faced blacks during those years. Many places didn't allow blacks to eat in the same places as whites. Blacks were not allowed to use the same water faucets and restrooms that whites used, and the list goes on.

Then in 1955, Rosa Parks, a 42-year-old black woman refused to give up her seat to a white man, which led to her arrest. This event happened in Montgomery, Alabama. She is often called the "mother of the modern-day civil rights movement.

Martin Luther King, Jr. became the leader of a group that formed to fight for civil rights. The group called the Montgomery Improvement Association that Dr. Marin Luther King, Jr. led, started a boycott of the buses in Montgomery that lasted almost 400 days.

Rosa Parks wasn't the only reason the movement took a more significant stance for justice. There was a young man named Emmett Till, who was hung by an angry white mob just because he was talking to a white girl.

Dr. Martin Luther King Jr., only promoted peaceful protest and never just limited the movement to black only as stated before.

I still can remember seeing Dr. Martin Luther Jr. hit by a rock while peacefully marching in Marquette Park in 1966. I remember seeing the violent beatings as black people tried to cross the Edmund Pettus Bridge in Alabama, which is now known as Bloody Sunday, all while still marching peacefully. Even if you don't like the movement, you have to admire the brave souls of those who took such abuse and didn't retaliate.

These events sparked national outrage of how blacks were being treated and caused many of the laws that protect people's rights of all colors and creeds today.

The "I have a dream" speech that Dr. Martin Luther King, Jr. gave, showed no animosity or hatred toward anyone. It only spoke of equality for all. Below is the direct quotation of part of that speech that still gives me chills today and gives me the passion to fight for all people regardless of color or creed.

"Let us not wallow in the valley of despair, I say to you today, my friends. And so even though we face the difficulties of today and tomorrow, I still have a dream. It is a dream deeply rooted in the American dream. I have a dream that one day this nation will rise up and live out the true meaning of its creed: "We hold these truths to be self-evident, that all men are created equal." I have a dream that one day on the red hills of Georgia, the sons of former slaves and the sons of former slave owners will be able to sit down together at the table of brotherhood. I have a dream that one day even the state of Mississippi, a state sweltering with the heat of injustice, sweltering with the heat of oppression, will be transformed into an oasis of freedom and justice. I have a dream that my four little children will one day live in a nation where they will not be judged by the color of their skin but by the content of their character. I have a *dream* today! I have a dream that one day, down in Alabama, with its vicious racists, with its governor having his lips dripping with the words of "interposition" and "nullification" -- one day right there in Alabama, little black boys and black girls will be able to join hands with little white boys and white girls as sisters and brothers. I have a *dream* today!"

With all the laws that were passed to protect the black people and give them equality, I feel this movement was necessary because many places were not honoring the equality and freedom that should be given to everyone in America.

As can happen in any movement, however, there were people who used this opportunity to incite violence and destruction as a way to make their voices heard. The main leader of that group was Malcomb X. However, even Malcomb X surrendered to Dr. Martin Luther Jr.'s approach to non-violence as the right way to get the message heard.

In my opinion, one of the best things that came out of this movement was the Civil Rights Act of 1964. In this law, it ended segregation and stopped discrimination in employment when it came to race, color, religion, sex, or national origin.

What I love most about this law is that it didn't cover just a particular race or group. It was for ALL people in the United States to be able to use for protection.

Two things, however, were a problem. One, if you noticed in history, some people didn't obey the law that was passed and was still being discriminatory toward people. The other, it also caused reverse discrimination due to the fear that companies might be charged with being discriminatory if they didn't hire the right amount of people in a certain race, religion, or other factors the law was intended to protect.

Laws can be useful, but they must be fair, and they must be enforced without any prejudice. On the flip side, it is dangerous to allow a government to pass too many laws to try to enforce individual behavior. That will never work. You can never pass enough laws to stop people who are bent on causing trouble or hurting people. Passing too many laws only gives the government too much power in which they can, in turn, use the same rules to blind us as to protect us.

Don't ever fall for the lie that big government is there for our benefit. As Lord Action once said, "Power tends to corrupt; absolute power corrupts absolutely." We are seeing this more and more to be true in our government leaders today.

Major Movements from the '50S -'70S

In the years from the '50s through the '70s, America went through a lot of changes. It seemed that changes were taking place daily. People all over were coming against our standard values concerning war, sex, religion, government policies, and more.

In this section, I will hit the highlights of some of the biggest movements that were taking place during those years.

As with every movement, some good came out of it, but consequently, some bad did as well. It is my personal belief that anytime we change laws that destroy our moral or family values, there will be problems that arise from it. It's not always clear if the good outweighs the bad until many years later.

I will be giving my personal opinions on some of these actions. You may or may not agree with me, which is your right as an American. I only hope and pray that each and every one of us can continue to voice our opinions with the freedom of speech we have in this nation for many years to come.

The Gay Civil Rights Movement

Under this movement, its main goals were to give equal rights to gay men, lesbians, transgender people or bisexuals. They wanted those rights to protect them in housing, applying for credit, and also any unfair treatment in the workplace or for employment.

I want to point out that one of the first gay rights groups founded was in 1950 by Harry Hay and another founder, Dale Jennings. It was called the Mattachine Foundation. However, the first organization can be traced as far back as 1924. Jennings later also formed another organization called One Inc., which allowed women and also started the country's first pro-gay magazine.

It is interesting also to note, both men eventually were removed from these organizations due to their affiliation with communism. Jennings was even arrested once for solicitation and only was released due to a hung jury. To me, an organization is only as good as its founder.

It was during this same time, around 1952, that the American Psychiatric Association labeled homosexuality as a type of mental disorder. If you say homosexuality is a mental disorder today, you will most likely be thrown into jail because of hate speech.

When Dwight D. Eisenhower banned gay people or people of sexual perversion in 1953 from holding positions in federal jobs, this help create a reason to fight for equal rights laws in the workplace.

During those early years, gays and lesbians were mistreated, not allowed in some bars, beaten, not allowed in the military, and such, which also made the push for equal rights laws to protect them.

A law called "Don't Ask, Don't Tell" was passed so that gays could be in the military under President Bill Clinton in 1992. The basic idea was that if you were gay, don't mention it, and you would be allowed to serve in the armed forces. This law was repealed by President Obama in 2011.

One of the most notable landmarks in the gay movement was "The Stonewall Riots," where police went to an inn called Stonewall that welcomed all forms of the gay lifestyle and began beating the people inside. What followed was five days of riots

.

One year later, many took to the street in a march to honor that day. That is now called the Gay Pride Parade, and that also is when the pink triangle symbol started for the gay pride.

To me, one of the laws that was passed to protect can bring more harm than good. It was called "The Hate Crime Law." This law was passed in 1994. It allowed the court to give people a harder punishment who came against the gay lifestyle. President Obama extended the original law to provide more power to the states in 2009. This law was brought about because of the pistol-whipping and torture of Matthew Shepard, who was openly gay. He later died of those injuries.

In 2015, the Supreme Court allowed gay marriages. In 2017, the Boy Scouts began allowing gays for leaders and workers. Ironically, this brought on a lawsuit against the Boy Scouts because of several cases of inappropriate sexual behavior within the Scouts. Both the Boy Scouts and the Girl Scouts also lifted bans, which now allowed transgender people of each sex. From there, we have gone as far as allowing transgender people in our public restrooms.

You might not think that any of this can bring problems, but trust me, it will. First of all, I do believe that all people should be treated fairly in our nation. No one person or race should have any more rights than any other. That said, however, there must be boundaries set in place to protect people from the very laws that were created to protect a class of people.

Although I don't agree with the homosexual lifestyle, I should not expect them to live their lives according to my principle. I do, however, expect the right to believe and lead my family in the direction I feel is right without the fear of punishment, threats, or intimidation.

I won't even go into the argument whether or not a person is born gay or not, thus giving them the rights to their actions. I've heard the case "I was born that way." I was born heterosexual, but that doesn't give me the right to have sex with every person I can of the opposite sex. I still must use constraint. Either way, I will not stand in front of a person's right to live a lifestyle that they choose as long as it doesn't interfere with another person's rights.

Here are a few of the problems I have with the laws that have been passed and how they can cause us trouble in the future and even today.

On the hate crime bill, I agree wholeheartedly with protecting anyone from discrimination or bodily harm. That all should fall under one law to protect ALL people.

The problem that is being faced today, however, is they are pushing that law to include hate speech. There should never be allowed laws that govern our freedom of speech. I understand that the old cliché "sticks and stones may break my bones, but words will never harm me" is not true. Words do hurt. Words can break you, but once again, you can never pass laws that will protect people from being hurt by words. When you try to do that, you silence anyone from their own beliefs and ideas at any given moment, thus controlling their God-given freedom.

I am a white man. You have your right, and I will defend your right to call me "white privileged," a "honky", "white trash," or anything else you desire. What you call me will never define who I am. I am who I say I am. Only I know my heart and why I believe as I do.

Instead of passing laws to stop our speech, we need to spend more on mental help so people with weak minds that can't handle being called names can get the help they need, not silence the peoples' voice.

You can mark my words. Governing our freedom of speech will lead to communism faster than you can imagine. It is only a matter of time until preachers will be thrown in jail or worse because they preached a sermon dealing with homosexuality as the Bible teaches it. It will be labeled as a hate crime.

This then will lead to the control of our religious freedom. The powers that be are already trying to label fundamental Christians as a terrorist group. So with the passing of just one law, two of our fundamental freedoms in America are being threatened. And if you recall, the communist admits that to take down a country, you must remove its family structure and its religion.

It is breaking down the family values and structure by allowing people to say they are one sex when, in reality, they are not. Your words don't determine your sex; your sexual organs do, duh. You may feel and act more like the opposite sex, but you are what you were born with.

By passing laws that allow transgenders to go into either restroom or get into the different organizations like the Boys and Girl Scouts, it opens the door for sexual perverts that want to harm children or rape women to say they are transgender but, in reality, have alternative motives in mind.

Once again, I am all for protecting the rights of others no matter who they are or what they believe as long as it doesn't impose on the rights of others. I am glad for the LGBT to gain the same rights as far as housing, jobs, protection against bodily harm, and such, but not to the extent of making me change my lifestyle to accommodate theirs. And the same would go for them to me.

If you feel you should go into the opposite sex's restroom because of your identity in your mind of what you are, get a sex change; they are available. Then you can truly be who you say you are.

The other problem I am having with this today is the fact that sexual behavior is being taught to our young children, and they are telling them that if they feel gay, they are. That is a lie straight from hell.

First of all, it is not the school's job to teach my children what is acceptable behavior. That is interfering with my rights to govern my own family. They are systematically trying to change America's belief on family and sex to make it appear that ALL sexual acts are good and acceptable. This will end in a catastrophe.

Secondly, just because you feel an attraction to the same sex doesn't make you gay! It is a proven fact that when we begin to get a rush on our hormones, we become very sexually driven. That can lead to wanting and desiring the opposite sex or same-sex. But during that period of time in one's life, it is not a determining factor of your sexual preference but rather an act brought on by hormones.

We should teach our kids it's ok to feel those things during the changes of their bodies but wait to have sexual intercourse until your mind and body are fully developed so you can make a wise choice, and that choice shouldn't be prodded along by the school system. It is normal behavior to have those thoughts of desiring the same sex during the change of life, not a time for identifying who you are. And yes, I still think they should be taught abstinence until marriage.

My point here is this, leave childrens' upbringing to the parents, and leave our rights of freedom of speech and religion alone. Stop trying to conform the nation to your own ideology and allow ALL Americans the freedom to choose and believe as they wish without stopping your beliefs. There is so much more to be said here on how this is being used to destroy America, but we must move on.

The Counterculture Movement

The counterculture movement had just about everything you can imagine in it that revolted against

America and the American value system. It was a time to "express yourself."

The movement started in the '60s, and in my opinion, it was mainly brought about with the American youth coming against the Vietnam War. I would say it reached its peak around 1969.

This movement changed or at least confronted anything traditional. The vast majority were anti-war, anti-consumerist and wanted a change. It was ironic they were resistant to spending, and yet it was because of the good economy they had the funds to spend time demonstrating.

Through this movement, the sexual revolution, women's rights, (which included having women change their ideas about the roles they played in the home), the gay movement, and other racial movements were all born, in one way or another.

The hippies were recognized as the longest part of the movement. They embraced sex, drugs, and rock-n-roll to express themselves. They also had the media in their favor because, like today, the media loves to stir the pot of anything that is going on.

Out of this movement, some of the best-known music artists formed, which helped the movement by the lyrics they sang in their songs. From psychedelic rock to pop art, things were changing. People like "The Beatles," "The Grateful Dead," "The Rolling Stones," Janis Joplin," and "Jimmy Hendrix are some that led the pack.

The counterculture movement was the era when the iconic Woodstock Music Festival was born. Four days of rock and psychedelic music from 32 artists with over half a million people were a part of it in New York.

The lyrics in the songs promoted free, open sex, drugs, and rebellion against authority. Songs like "Light My Fire," "Sex, Drugs and Rock and Roll," and "Age of Aquarius" filled the air as the spectators took their dope, danced in the nude, and open sex was the norm. The aftermath left a ton of trash that had to be cleaned up by the locals. Many of the people at the event even used peoples' property to relieve their bowels.

It was also the start of the New Age religion and other forms of worship that wasn't a part of America's culture. They were looking for answers for things they couldn't understand.

Many of the people in the movement lived in communes, and most of them were young. They would hold public protests, cause campus uprisings, and practiced sexual liberation with no holds barred.

Although the movement started to dwindle by the '70s, the effects and still some of the results are alive and well today. Many also were environmentalists or what was called at the time, "tree huggers." One thing for sure, it changed America forever and not necessarily for the good.

Black Lives Matter Movement

I feel the next four movements have done more to divide America and destroy its freedom more than any other actions in the history of America.

For this reason, I have spent much more time covering these. I will not go into the conspiracies that I am sure most have read on social media. But instead, I will try my best to do as an old detective series that was on television called "Dragnet" did. One of the main phrases on the show was spoken by a detective talking to witnesses, and he would say,

"Just the facts ma'am, just the facts." That is what we will try to do. Present just the facts.

One of the current and most televised movements in America is the Black Lives Matter movement. But before I begin, I would like to explain a little more about me and what I believe.

The reason I want to do this is that many will say that I am looking at things through a white man's eyes or that I am prejudiced toward blacks, but that is far from the truth. Just for the record, the reason I use the term black is that not every black person in America came from Africa, so I won't classify them as African American.

When I just started elementary school, blacks were beginning to be bussed to better school districts so they could get a better education. I felt that it was a good thing and still do today.

Many times, however, I found myself bullied by some of the blacks. They would take my lunch, take ribbons that I won during field day, or just try to intimidate me.

I didn't allow that to make me hate blacks because my father taught me to treat everyone with respect.

We knew that the actions of a few were not the reflection of all. And I also had quite a few precious black friends in school.

After I was grown and had my own family, my daughter was raped by a 22-year-old black male when she was only 12. As a result, it will be hard for her to understand what true love is or what pure sex is for the rest of her life. This man continued to have sex with her for the next few years, unknown to us, until she got pregnant.

Once I found out what this man did and how old this person was, it didn't matter what color, it was the action that took place, I wanted justice. I wanted to see this man go to prison for the mandatory 20 years that is the punishment for statutory rape.

The case never made it to court. To my surprise, this man was not charged at all for the rape. The charges were dropped as a plea bargain on other things he had done in the past. I was both shocked and very angry with the justice system that would allow such a man to go free.

It wasn't long after that, this same man called me and said, " I know I am the last person you would ever want to talk to, but I really need advice in my life, and I believe you are the only one I know that will give me the truth."

My first thought was, HELL NO. But my spirit saw a man whose life was ruined and was looking for a way to change. For that reason, I allowed him to come over.

To make a long story short, he confessed everything in his life. He told how miserable and sorry he was for those actions and wanted guidance on how to change.

I told him the exact truth, which I am sure was hard for him to hear, but he listened and took my advice. He told me how appreciative he was for my honesty and said he never had a male figure to talk to him that way. He asked if he could continue to call for advice, and I let him know he could.

I mentioned all of this to show I don't look at the color. I look at actions and why people do what they do. I am willing to help and be friends with anyone. I have several black friends I consider family. We have blacks, mixed races, and all in our biological family. I know there are good and evil in ALL races, including white. So please try and remember, as you read these hard statements that follow, it is coming from the actions and truth, not a race.

When you read the Black Lives Matter Manifesto, it doesn't sound all that bad on the surface. On some of the points, they even include all people, including sexual orientation and practice. But when you see the actions, it becomes clear it is more about creating a black nation, civil unrest, and division in America.

According to the movement, they are non-violent and just trying to get justice and equal treatment as anyone else and to let their voices and concerns be heard. But is this the case? Do they really oppose using violence to be heard? Let's take a look at the starting of the movement, why it started, and the founders of this movement, and maybe we can get a better understanding. This will take some time because I want to use all of the very examples they have used to move this agenda forward.

The movement started back in 2013, stemming from the death of Trayvon Martin, a 17-year-old black youth that was killed by George Zimmerman, a security officer. According to their assessment of the situation, Martin was just coming home from a store late at night and was confronted by Zimmerman. Zimmerman began to harass Martin, questioning why he was out so late. The altercation eventually left unarmed Martin dead by the actions of Zimmerman, and yet Zimmerman was acquitted.

The incident created an outcry from the black community, demanding justice. If that wasn't bad enough, in 2014, two more supposedly innocent black men were killed by the police. Michael Brown was shot, allegedly with his hands up, saying, "don't shoot," and Tamir Rice, a teen boy, was shot even though supposedly unarmed. Eric Garner also died from an illegal choke hold by a police officer. The four of these sparked riots and looting all over the nation.

These are not by far the first incidences of black men being beaten or killed by police officers. But most have not been in the media as much as the above. Along with the Rodney King beating in 1991 by L.A. police officers, up until that time. What made matters worse with the Rodney King beating was the mainly white jury acquitted the officers that did it.

The Rodney King beating was one of the first that showed a video of the beating by the police officers. With modern-day technology and almost everyone owning a cell phone, it is becoming common practice to video police while making an arrest. Riots also came out of the jury's decision by the black community. Two of the officers were eventually charged, and King was awarded $3.8 million dollars in a civil trial because of the beating he received.

And then recently, George Floyd was killed supposedly by an officer cutting off his breathing. Then, Rayshard Brooks, who was another supposedly unarmed man shot by police and killed. Both incidences were filmed by cell phones during the altercation.

George Floyd and Rayshard Brooks' deaths have sparked riots, looting, and racial tension for months now in 2020.

On the surface, I believe looking at these men and the way the videos and stories portray the events would bring an outcry for change from every American citizen. And rightfully so.

According to the movement, blacks are being targeted by the police department and systematically killed off. That would bring fear to any race of people. Just imagine the pandemonium that must have broken out when the Jews realized that Hitler was rounding them all up to be put to death! How could this happen in today's civilization, especially in America! The land of the free!

As mentioned, the fear that the black community was being killed by police was the motivation to start the Black Lives Matter movement, or so they say.

The organization was founded by three black women, Alicia Garza, Patrice Cullors, and Opal Tometi, in 2013. So, for such a massive movement that has impacted so significantly, it is relatively new. The movement has now become worldwide.

All three of these women are organizers; two are writers and freedom fighters or activists. Patrice Cullors has admitted that she and the other two are "trained Marxists" and that the movement is founded on that principle.

Cullors doesn't seem to have a problem with identifying with the communist party and considers the work of the Black Panther Party a "great work," as she was a trained organizer with the Labor/Community Strategy Center, which stands for, and is based upon, the statements mentioned above.

She was taught or trained, according to the New York Post, under the ideas of Eric Mann. He, for the record, created the Students for a Democratic Society from which Bill Ayers and Bernadine Dohrn splintered to form the Weather Underground. This organization tried to overthrow the United States and, in 1969, was classified as a domestic terror organization by the FBI. Oh, and by the way, four years ago, Charles Wade was in the movement as well. His job was to supply housing and help fund protestors. He just recently was charged with human trafficking and underage prostitution.

If you ask me, those are some strange bedfellows to be snuggling up to if you stand for freedom and America. Because of this, it made me think just how legit the movement was for America. I wondered if anything was misrepresented to push a communist agenda.

We have already seen through the information supplied by the former KGB Yuri Bezmenov and FBI agent W. Cleon Skousen how communists work. They use people, labor, and movements to derail America, to deceive people into believing a lie, thus creating a crisis. And then when Black Lives Matter began to cry for the defunding of the police…a light bulb came on!

Let's now take a closer look at the facts of these allegations against police officers. Are all cops out to wipe the black people off? Are they truly targets, or are the incidents more the results of the ones being arrested than about the arresting officers?

With cell phone videos to back the accusers' stories, it would seem to be an open and shut case. However, the same is true as what is called a half-truth. A half-truth is still a whole lie, and unless the video shows start to finish, it can't be trusted as fact, as you will soon see.

The biggest problem in America today is that we take a half-truth and form our judgment accordingly. All of the officers on all the cases mentioned above were, by the public, tried, and condemned without due process of law. People weren't concerned with the facts, just "justice." But how can you have true justice without facts? It's impossible.

For this reason, I went back to see the trial facts so we can determine if these men were acting out of prejudice against the victims, or did the victims have a significant role in the final outcome of their demise.

The best place to start is with the first person mentioned, Trayvon Martin. It was true that Trayvon

Martin was unarmed. It was true that Zimmerman confronted and started questioning Martin as to why he was out so late. But what the media did, was change the perspective of the people by showing a picture of Trayvon when he was only 13 or 14 years old.

This made Martin look like a small framed, happy-go-lucky young male. They used the arrest photo of Zimmerman. The arrest photo made Zimmerman look like a bully and power-hungry man. The fact was, Martin was at the time of the incident 5'11" and 158 lbs. with a football player build, and Zimmerman was 5'7" and 204 lbs. with a chubby build.

The other thing mentioned was that Martin attacked and beat Zimmerman before Zimmerman made the first shot. The pathologist confirmed that from the injuries Zimmerman received, it was consistent with the story that Zimmerman was attacked and beaten first, leaving his head bleeding.

So at the least, Martin was not the small-sized boy that did nothing that might have caused his death. Had he not attacked Zimmerman, he might still be alive today. There was enough evidence in the case to prove Zimmerman could have acted in self-defense. It is a sad thing that Martin was shot and killed, but we must all take responsibility for our actions that may lead to our demise. To me, this would not have been a case that I would have used to start a movement to end hate crimes.

Next, let's look at Michael Brown. This case made such an impact on the nation, that not only did it help start the Black Lives Matter movement, but two of our democratic leaders made official statements on the fifth-year anniversary of his death supporting the movement. Here are their direct quotes.

Kamala Harris (running for vice president in 2020) tweeted, "Michael Brown's murder forever changed Ferguson and America. His tragic death sparked a desperately needed conversation and a nationwide movement. We must fight for stronger accountability and racial equity in our justice system."

Elizabeth Warren tweeted, "5 years ago, Michael Brown was murdered by a white police officer in Ferguson, Missouri. Michael was unarmed, yet he was shot six times. I stand with activists and organizers who continue the fight for justice for Michael. We must confront systemic racism and police violence head-on."

To gain this much support and recognition by our government leaders, surely the facts must show there was a problem with social injustice in the case, right? Especially since one was a prosecutor and the other a law professor.

Think again. In this case, as mentioned earlier, Michael Brown was reportedly shot with both hands raised, saying, "Don't shoot." If we only listen to the media's side of this, it should be an open and shut case. NO ONE should be shot by the police while their hands are raised! That would clearly be Murder!

Supposedly the whole thing started when Brown went over a store counter, stole some cigarettes, and shoved the store owner. Officers were alerted. Officer Wilson responded, and during the confrontation, Wilson shot the unarmed man six times.

But contrary once again to all the media hype, everything is not what it seems. What was proven in a court of law that the media doesn't want people to know is that DNA showed Brown's DNA on the officer's collar, shirt, and pants. Kind of hard to do with your hands in the air, don't you think? Further, more DNA showed the officer's DNA on Brown's palm. Once again, hard to do with your hands raised, and it also shows a sign of struggle.

When dealing with an officer shooting a person, you have to look at the local laws that warrant the right to shoot as well. In Missouri, where the incident took place, the code reads as follows: "In effecting an arrest or in preventing an escape from custody, a law enforcement officer is justified in using deadly force … when the officer reasonably believes that such use of deadly force is immediately necessary to effect the arrest or prevent an escape from custody and also reasonably believes that the person to be arrested … is attempting to escape by use of a deadly weapon or dangerous instrument." So the officer was well in his right to shoot. We might not agree with the law, but we have to live by it. So yet again, this is another case where resisting arrest played a factor in a person's death.

In the Tamir Rice case, a 12-year-old black child was shot and killed by an officer in Ohio. I watched the video of this one. And there is no doubt that Rice was shot and killed by the officers. But let us look at why the shooting occurred.

On November 22, 2014, Rice was outside playing with a toy gun. Someone reported to the police that a child was waving a gun around and pointing it at people. The caller supposedly did say at the beginning and middle of the call, that the gun might be fake. However, we are not sure that the dispatcher gave that information to the responding officers or not. The event took place at the Cudell Recreation Center in Cleveland.

The officers arrived at the scene quickly and rushed out of their cars. When the officers arrived, one of the officers saw Rice put the gun in his waistband. Immediately the officers cried out from the patrol car for Rice to put his hands up, and then also, when they got out of the car they told him to show his hands.

Instead, Rice, without saying a word, reached for the toy gun in his waistband and began to pull it out. At that point, the officer shot Rice two times, killing the boy.

This is indeed a tragic story, but it doesn't fit the bill of a police shooting without a cause. In the first place, the officers knew the suspect was armed but didn't know it was a toy gun. This already makes police officers on high alert, and they will respond quickly and forcefully right away when they feel threatened.

Secondly, Rice didn't respond to the police officer's orders. Here again, this makes police on edge and are expecting resistance and possibly a fight.

Finally, Rice reached for his gun. At that point, the officers had a split second to respond, and they responded by firing two justifiable shots. It needs to be noted as well that the toy gun looked exactly like a real 9mm. You would never know the difference between the two from just a foot away.

To show how quickly things happened, it was only 2 seconds after the officers got out of the car and Rice was shot. Parents, please, please, please, no matter your race, tell your kids to do what the officers are telling you to do. If they are in the wrong, you can have your day in court, but you will live to be able to do so. You adults need to heed the same rule.

Although this is a tragic event, it still hasn't proven that cops are out to kill black people, but rather are responding to situations where the victims are resisting orders given to deescalate the situation.

Eric Garner died after an officer put an illegal choke-hold on him. He was only being arrested for selling cigarettes without a license. With just those facts, I believe the actions of the officer may have crossed the line.

The first problem that initially caused the choke-hold at the start was Garner resisting the arresting officer and yelling, "don't touch me."

No matter how small the offense is, officers have a sworn duty to arrest a person committing a crime. It is the responsibility of the person being arrested to cooperate with the officers' demands. By doing so, your chance of being injured or killed during an arrest goes substantially down. It's common sense, folks!

Yes, the choke-hold was banned, but it also was the one that the officer was taught while in training. That may not be an excuse for using the hold, but to say that the hold was what caused Garner's death is not completely true.

Garner weighed 350 lbs. Even for his height of 6'3," that is still considered overweight. Because of this, he suffered heart disease, sleep apnea, severe asthma, and diabetes, which all contributed to his death and may have played a more significant part since he was pronounced dead an hour later from a heart attack.

He also wasn't what we call a model citizen, with over 30 arrests which included assault and grand theft. Officers sometimes know the background of the individual from dispatch or now from their personal computers in the car. This makes them more aware of who they are dealing with and what may come of it.

Now we have reached the Rodney King incident. This man was videotaped being beaten brutally at the hands of white police officers, and another officer kicking him. Of course, the media made sure to show all of this and point out that it was done at the hands of white police officers. But they only used the last half of the tape to make their assumption.

Because of the half-truth, full lie shown, it sparked riots and destruction that left $800 million dollars in property damage, and 53 people lost their lives. I still have the image of a group of black people surrounding a truck driver as he was trying to get through the mob. They yanked him out of the cab, threw him on the ground, beat him unmercifully, and then threw a brick at his head.

As he lay there half dead, the mob jumped around, shouting and dancing around his body. My question then and still is now, why should people who didn't cause the problem and their property suffer because of the acts of other individuals? Those actions that took place after the Rodney King beating are nothing more than animalistic, and all should be brought to justice! That innocent man and the others killed did not deserve what came to them. Most were just trying to get home to a family after a hard day's work while these low-life thugs caused havoc and fear.

I blame most of these destructive actions on the media for only showing half of the video. It was true that King hadn't done much wrong in his life. He only had one felony, and that was a result of him being drunk. He did have a problem with alcohol though.

What the video didn't show was King, while intoxicated, flying down the expressway at speeds of 115 MPH. This alone is a danger to anyone that may have been on the road at the time. I guess innocent lives killed at the hands of a drunk driver don't matter though, do they?

After King stopped, the officers tried to arrest him without being aggressive, but King resisted. They even tried to stop him with a taser gun that didn't do the job. This led the officers to believe he was high on something, so they jumped him. King pushed them off like it was nothing. King then charged the officers. It was at the point that officers began to beat him with the batons to gain control.

So, once again, was it worth the lives of 53 people and 800 million dollars of property damage to fight for a person who brought all of this on himself by resisting arrest and breaking the law? If so, our country is really messed up in its thinking.

This brings us to our most recent people who were killed by the police, George Floyd and Rayshard Brooks.

As most of you probably know, the death of George Floyd brought on the well-known phrase, "I can't breathe," which became a part of the Black Lives Matter movement.

Out of all of the cases so far mentioned, in my opinion, George Floyd has more validity than the others when it comes to abuse of power by the police. But that is not to say it squarely lies on the police only.

The video that surfaced shows plainly George Floyd being held down by a cop's knee for over 8 minutes, and Floyd saying he couldn't breathe. According to the coroner's report, the cause of death, it was from asphyxiation and Floyd didn't resist arrest.

Floyd's crimes in the past were mainly charges of having or intending to sell drugs, trespassing, theft, and one charge of aggravated robbery with a deadly weapon. This, compared to today's crimes, doesn't seem that major.

But even in the George Floyd case, there are still things that need to be exposed to have the full truth. It was reported and videoed that Floyd didn't resist arrest; however, another video finally emerged that showed him not fully complying with the officers' commands when getting him out of the car. He also was filmed trying to resist getting in the patrol car, claiming he was claustrophobic.

The video is hard to watch because it is evident that Floyd is afraid, with no apparent reason, of the officers at the beginning. And it is possible that his claustrophobic condition brought on the panic attack, which led him to resist getting in the patrol car. But all that being said, you still must obey the orders that are being given to you for your and the patrol officers' safety. I can't emphasize that enough. The officers don't know you, your health issues, or your mental state, so they will respond in a manner that will ensure their and the publics' safety.

We all know what happened next. That was when Floyd was held down almost 9 minutes by the knee of the cop even after he became unconscious. But was that the full cause of his death?

Although the examiner previously said it was a homicide, he also said he died from a cardiopulmonary arrest event that could have been brought on by the restraint. However, the findings later revealed that there was no physical support of asphyxiation. Other health problems such as heart disease and toxins in his blood combined with the restraint are what caused his death. Fentanyl, Norfentanyl, Methamphetamine, and THC were all found in his bloodstream at the time of his death. All these combined are what actually caused his death.

Nancy Pelosi gave an American flag to honor George Floyd as being another African American killed or beaten by police officers. This has nothing to do with flags that are given to vets. Although Floyd's past may not have been that bad and maybe his resisting arrest was out of fear, as well as having mental and physical conditions, it still to me didn't warrant having a funeral with such honor and parade including a 24-carat gold casket. I believe those types of honor should be given to people who have sacrificed their lives or done something that is positive for the nation, not just for a person who although sad and misfortunate, died while being arrested, however sad and un-fortunate.

Last but not least on our list is the killing of Rayshard Brooks by a police officer. This event started with officers responding to a person in Wendy's drive-through that was passed out from being intoxicated. There was a partial video of this showing the time that Rayshard Brooks was shot, his back turned toward the police officer. But as with all the stories so far, there was more in play.

From information gathered by witnesses, they said Brooks was begging for the officers to let him go home. That's all he wanted to do was go home to be with his wife and kids to celebrate his child's birthday.

When the officers were about to arrest Brooks for DUI, a scuffle began. Brooks was able to get away from the officer taking the officer's taser gun with him. As they were chasing him, the officer shot him in the back, and then one of the officers said, "I got him," and afterward, kicked Brooks after he had been shot.

According to police reports, however, and video, there was a scuffle while trying to arrest Brooks. Brooks threw both officers off of him with ease and grabbed one of the officer's taser gun and punched one of the officers. As the officers chased Brooks, Brooks made a half turn and shot the taser at the officer. The other officer then dropped his taser, pulled his gun, and shot Brooks once in the back and once in the buttocks. Brooks died from those injuries.

It is true as far as it can be confirmed that the officer said, "I got him" after he shot Brooks, and one of the officers did kick him while he was on the ground after being shot.

What happened to Brooks sparked rage in Atlanta, which led to riots, burning down the Wendy's, and vandalizing and looting businesses and property. Some of the protesters during the days of riots were armed and blocking roads. One of the events left an 8-year-old black girl dead from being shot while her parent was trying to go around the roadblock.

All of this could have been avoided had Brooks only surrendered to the cops without resisting. More information came out about Brooks later on that showed his checkered past.

The media has made Brooks look like a hard-working family man and an upright citizen, but court arrest records shine another light on that. The Hemingway Report released Brooks' criminal past records, and these are the crimes that were listed in the report; simple battery, cruelty to children, false imprisonment, family violence battery, receiving stolen property, criminal interference with government property, weapons charges, and obstructing a law enforcement officer in the preceding years.

It went on to say that Brooks may have fled Ohio because of charges. And as far as being a good family man, Brooks told the cops he wanted to go home to be with his wife and kids. That may have been true that night, but the news found out later that Brooks had a girlfriend. She was charged with starting the fire that burned down Wendy's restaurant after he was shot. Not to mention the fact, if your goal was to be home with your wife and kids, why are you passed out drunk?

According to the Hemmingway Report, it also mentioned that Brooks might have resisted because another arrest could have brought him hard time in prison. As you see, things aren't always what they seem to be.

So, with each and every one of the people that the BLM uses to protest against police brutality toward blacks, all of them started by someone resisting arrest or not doing what the officers told them to do. EVERY ONE OF THEM.

It is because of these false and deceptive reports that blacks are fearing for their lives. I have talked to some of my personal black friends who have admitted that as young children, they were taught to be afraid of the police. They also said that they were taught they were only a black person and had no right to expect anything. Some of these teachings came from their parents.

This movement is based on total lies and deception. It is from these lies they are trying to defund, and quite frankly, dismantle the police department and, eventually, our military.

Don't get me wrong. Yes, in the '60s, blacks were treated very badly and had hardly any rights at all, including the right to vote. It is also true that there are cops that abuse their power and should be removed from office. But this is not the case with most officers. And it is not true that they are "killing off" black people.

According to Statista 2020, these are the total deaths by police shootings by race. In 2017- 457 whites, 223 blacks, 179 Hispanics, 44 other, and 84 unknown. In 2018- 399 whites, 209 blacks, 148 Hispanics, 36 other, and 202 unknown. In 2019- 370 whites, 235 blacks, 158 Hispanic, 39 other, and 202 unknown. 2020- 215 whites, 111 blacks, 71 Hispanic, 15 other, and 146 unknown.

The black population, according to the census bureau, in 2020 is around 57.8 million, the white population is approximately 308 million, and from what I could gather, there are nearly 700,000 police officers.

In this same year, there have been around 215 whites killed by police, 111 blacks killed by police, and so far over 29 cops killed by shootings alone. Out of these killings of whites and blacks, 97% of the victims were armed during the shooting.

When you put all this in perspective and the fact that officers have to make split-second decisions under stress, most of the time knowing the individual is armed and dangerous, I don't think these numbers show that cops are trying to "kill off" any group of people, coupled with the fact that most of these people were shot because of resistance or not following orders.

It should also be noted, according to the federal database, there is an arrest every three seconds in the US. With that many arrests and the low numbers of all races being killed during the arrest, it shows even less reason to believe there is a real systematic problem with law enforcement.

The other thing that bothers me about blacks being afraid of the cops is that here in Atlanta, every day, you see blacks going over 90 MPH on the roads. They also are shutting down the freeways to do doughnuts, and driving ATV's right past the police and even mocking them as they do it.

During the protests we have seen cameras around the U. S. s blacks throwing showing things at cops, spitting in their face, daring them to hit them, looting, burning down buildings, destroying cars, blocking highways, and more. These signs don't point to fear to me.

Now in saying all that, I am not saying that only blacks are doing these things. As a matter of fact, you will see under Antifa, that many races are involved. I only mention blacks because this movement is trying to center things as being unfair to blacks, and blacks are fearful because of it.

I also don't believe that these kinds of acts support the cause for change. Anyone doing these crimes should be punished no matter who they are or what race. Violence is not the proper reaction, no matter how mad you may be about something. It shows a lack of control and lack of respect for others and their property.

What makes matters worse is we have celebrities and people in our government that are bailing these people out of jail after committing such heinous crimes.

Can you not see there is more going on here than what they claim is justice? Isn't it interesting, too, that justice is not defined? What justice needs to be changed? Is it police crimes against blacks? Can't be. We just showed the numbers, and they don't add up. Or maybe it is because African Americans don't have the same opportunities as other Americans? Could that be it? Well, let's see some more statistics.

The BLM movement is pushing the agenda that blacks are unfairly treated and have an unfair position because of slavery and lack of help. They are even pushing the agenda of white privilege and that whites should have to give up their housing and money for blacks because of the slavery that took place over 155 years ago.

First, let me reemphasize that during the '60s and earlier, blacks were unfairly treated. I will also go as far as to say that the mindset thinking that was placed on them by society and their own people caused them to have a hard time climbing the ladder after the '60s. But to say they still have less advantage than other races in America today? I disagree.

According to "A Look at Historically Black Colleges and Universities as Howard turns 150", there are 101 historical black college universities in the United States. These were brought about mostly in 1964 and after due to the Civil Rights Act. According to the information, in 1965 special federal grants were given for those colleges called the Higher Education Act of 1965. Since that time, many other presidents of our nation added funding to these universities.

There are many grants available for the black community, not only for schools but for housing as well.

When I worked real estate actively, there were special loans given to minorities so they could afford better housing and in a better location. Also, laws have been passed that don't allow people to be discriminated against in the financing or where they choose to live. This gives a better advantage for minorities as any other race.

Laws have been passed to stop discrimination in hiring. The laws go as far as making it mandatory to hire a certain number of minorities even if someone else that is not a minority has more knowledge and skill for the same job.

Laws were made to be inclusive to all people, and if anyone strayed from those laws, he would be fined or jailed. However, the black community has its own Miss Black America and black entertainment awards (BET) to name just a couple. The list goes on with black only National Association of Black Journalists and National Conferences of Black Mayors and Elected Democrats. There is a Negro Dance organization. The Black Congressional Caucus, and far more. Believe me, if whites had any of these, there would be a tremendous outcry of racism.

Black actors have filed lawsuits against the movie industry about them not receiving enough rewards and have sued other businesses with similar ideas. People, this is not justice for all. It is reverse discrimination.

There may be some far and few things that are not equal between blacks and whites that are legit, but both sides have it. What it most of the time boils down to is, are you willing to work hard to achieve your goal?

There have been many blacks that have proven you can make it. They have not hung onto the poor mindset and the blame game about being slaves years ago. I love what Moran Freeman said, "If you want to stop racism stop talking about it."

If you are to use slavery as an excuse, what about the Jews? They have been enslaved more than any other group in the world. Yet, they work hard, never complain about their past, and work to rebuild their lives.

Or what about immigrants to this country. They come here not knowing anyone and having little or nothing but a dream, and because in America you can do anything you want, they work hard and make a great success in their dreams.

You can't blame your woes on things that happened over 100 years ago. Your success is up to you and your determination to achieve it. America never gave you the right to get things by the government. You have the right to life, liberty, and the PURSUIT of happiness." But it is up to you to work for it!

Since the '60s, there has been a fair share of black actors, business owners, teachers, police officers, mayors, governors, and even one being the president of the United States! Dr. Martin Luther King Jr. would never have dreamed the Civil Rights Movement would have taken blacks this far this soon.

Today, there are six black billionaires in the United States. Yes, I said billion, not million. That's impressive. And according to RichestBlacks.com, here are of the top ten richest blacks in America.
1. Robert F. Smith, CEO of Vista Equity Partners, worth $5 billion.

2. David Steward is worth $3 billion that he has made through investments..

3. Oprah Winfrey, whom we all know, is worth $2.5 billion.

4. Michael Jordan, pro basketball player, worth $1.9 billion.

5. Jay Z, rapper, worth $900 million

6. Sean Combs, another rapper and business entrepreneur, worth $825 million

7. Tiger Woods, pro golfer, worth $800 million

8. Tyler Perry, actor and now studio owner, worth $600 million

9. Robert Johnson, former owner of BET, worth $550 million.

10. Magc Johnson, basketball pro, worth $600 million.

Ask these people how they got their money. Ask them if it was just handed to them. Ask them if it came without a price. I can promise you, with every one of them the answer would be, I had a dream, and I worked my butt off to fulfill that dream.

I do feel sorry for the black population, however. The people have been used by our government as toys, and the government has kept them bound by the giveaway program. The black communities think these leaders want to help them, but if they did, they would make them self-sufficient in society, not oppressed.

Movements like the BLM have misled them to focus on their cause and agenda instead of teaching them the real facts of what is killing off the black population, which is black-on-black crimes.

They try and make the black population believe that their poverty is a direct result of whites and capitalism, and yet they don't point out that the reason black neighborhoods are full of burglar bars is not because of whites or anyone else but the blacks that live in their community. They are not taught that they have the opportunity to start their own business, to make their own success story.

They are not taught that 97% of black lives lost are from black hands. They are not taught that destroying businesses hurts their own community.

One of the saddest things I saw on television during all the protests, riots, and looting was an old black man crying in the street saying, "Why, why did you do this to my business. I have lived in the hood with you. Why have you done this to me?" From the age of that man, I doubt he will ever be able to recover from that.

As I mentioned at the beginning of this chapter, all three of the BLM founders are "trained Marxists." To crudely shorten the definition of a Marxist, they don't believe in capitalism and think that all wealth and property should be shared, so everyone is almost equal. They believe that capitalism divides people into rich and poor classes. To see how this movement thinks, it only takes reading what one of the founders wrote. Here is a list from BLM co-founder Chanelle Helm provided by Steve Macdonald:

Language Warning!

1. White people, if you don't have any descendants, will your property to a black or brown family. Preferably one that lives in generational poverty.
2. White people, if you're inheriting property you intend to sell upon acceptance, give it to a black or brown family. You're bound to make that money in some other white privileged way.
3. If you are a developer or realty owner of multi-family housing, build a sustainable complex in a black or brown blighted neighborhood and let black and brown people live in it for free.
4. White people, if you can afford to downsize, give up the home you own to a black or brown family. Preferably a family from generational poverty.

5. White people, if any of the people you intend to leave your property to are racist a**holes, change the will, and will your property to a black or brown family. Preferably a family from generational poverty.

6. White people, rebudget your monthly income so you can donate to black funds for land purchasing.

7. White people, especially white women (because this is yaw specialty — Nosey Jenny and Meddling Kathy), get a racist fired. Yaw know what the f*ck they be saying. You are complicit when you ignore them. Get your boss fired cause they racist too.

8. Backing up No. 7, this should be easy but all those sheetless Klan, Nazi's and Other lil' d*ck-white men will all be returning to work. Get they ass fired. Call the police even: they look suspicious.

9. OK, backing up No. 8, if any white person at your work, or as you enter in spaces and you overhear a white person praising the actions from yesterday, first, get a pic. Get their name and more info. Hell, find out where they work — Get Them Fired. But certainly address them, and, if you need to, you got hands: use them.

10. Commit to two things: Fighting white supremacy where and how you can (this doesn't mean taking up knitting, unless you're making scarves for black and brown kids in need), and funding black and brown people and their work.

The article further went to make a statement that Chanelle said she was only talking about people of non-color that could afford to do so and were willing to do so. However, knowing what philosophy they are trained in, that is highly doubtful. Furthermore, those were some of the racist comments I have heard for quite some time.

The reason I say it is questionable is that in another BLM protest in Chicago, an armed black man was shooting at police and was shot. As a result, looting and riots started. Ariel Atkins (a BLM leader) told the crowd that "many people are being evicted and dying, so why are we concerned about a few buildings being destroyed." She called it reparation because they deserve to take things so they can eat, and because of how they were treated. Then she goes on to down the police and says they don't need them.

Other militia groups are calling for the United States to give them a section of land that they can control all on their own inside of America but not part of America. They, too, are demanding reparation. And for those who don't really know what this new term "reparation" means, here is the definition: "the making of amends for a wrong one has done, by paying money to or otherwise helping those who have been wronged." Again, why should I be paying for something I had no part of and paying for something other people did wrong that went bad?

It is also to be noted that Marxism has a direct tie to communism. It is all based on the same notions. This whole give-me philosophy propaganda and dismantling the police all stem from this communist view and will be what destroys America.

The reason I have spent so much time on this movement is that this movement has acted out or at least encouraged the communist ideas and actions to change America. Below are a few examples.

They have used the tactic to come against law and order by defunding the police, attacking them, accusing them of abuse of power, and trying to dismantle them.

They have used the tactic to come against the power structure. They openly admit that one of their main goals is to come against President Trump and get him thrown out of office. They are against any form of government that is even remotely on the side of historical morals and values of America and are actively trying to get them removed from office.

They have used the tactic of disrupting social life by trying to divide the nation between blacks and whites. They are trying to use name-calling such as "White Supremacy" and White Privilege" to help bring this division.

They have used the labor tactic by making people believe that they are not being treated fairly in the workplace, that business owners are rich, careless, and greedy people and using workers as slaves to help them make more money. They never mention how much it costs to run a business, the extra taxes they pay, the additional cost in insurance, and the cost of the property and supplies.

They have used the education tactic by trying to remove history. They are actively trying to get every civil war statue, or anything related to it removed from the public and history.

And they have used the tactics of crisis and destabilization by trying to get people angry about how the blacks have been treated in the past and how people should pay for that over a hundred years later. They use fear tactics like the ones we saw in Portland and also in Stone Mountain ,GA when over 100 black

Militia took over the park, intimidating whites and making threats all while carrying assault rifles.

I could use so many more examples of how they have used all of these communist strategies to dismantle our nation and recreate one under socialistic and communistic patterns. I don't want to spend any more time showing how they are misleading people because it is plain to see they are using the very list that the communists have used. To me, this shows plainly, this isn't just about black lives matter.

ANTIFA

Another movement that is very dangerous and detrimental to America is Antifa. Unlike the Black Lives Matter Movement, this group is very open about using violence if it is needed. They also are admitted revolutionaries. What sets them apart from other movements is they have no real founder or leader but more scattered groups of people using the internet and other means of communication and to get their agenda out.

There is very little information about the group because it is not organized like any other significant movement with founding leaders and places but rather a mix of all types and beliefs. That is also one of the reasons that most of the time you will find them with their faces covered to keep from being identified. This can also be used to keep from getting in trouble with the law since cameras are everywhere now.

It is speculated that there are around 200-plus groups with different amounts of people in them and different types of actions they use. While writing this book, in Portland there have been over 75 days of protest. Portland and Minnesota seem to have had some of the worst destruction in these protests as well as LA. I find it amazing that in both Portland and Minneapolis, you see some of the largest based groups of Antifa.

Their actions are all about causing crisis, destruction, intimidation, and the use of violence, although they say violence is not their primary tool to bring change. In my opinion, if there ever was a group that should be listed as a domestic terrorist group, it would be Antifa. Our government has been petitioned by many trying to get them classified as such. But according to our government, they are bound by laws that prevent them from being able to do so.

We saw them for the first time that we know of when President Trump was elected. They literally hate Trump and anyone that supports him. They have been known to attack supporters of Trump physically because, in their mind, anyone that supports him is a fascist.

They are against the far-right extremists, white supremacists, or any racists; however, they mix themselves in groups like the Black Lives Matter so they can cause havoc and destruction.

Here is a direct quote from Wikipedia where most of this information comes from. "Individuals involved in the movement tend to hold anti-authoritarian and anti-capitalist views, subscribing to a range of left-wing ideologies such as anarchism, communism, Marxism, social democracy, and socialism. Both the name Antifa and the logo with two flags representing anarchism and communism are derived from the German Antifa movement."

Antifa didn't start in the past few years. They have been around with the same ideology, although not necessarily called Antifa, since the 1920s. It appears most of the people involved in the early years were from Italy who fought against the Italian dictator Benito Mussolini, who was a fascist.

By the 1980s, they roamed with skinheads and punk rockers to help deter people from joining the Klan and other hate groups. Mark Bray quoted them as saying, "We go where they go." This was to signify that wherever there were people with right-winged thinking, they would be there to try and stop them no matter where it was.

They have used racism as their fight against fascism with the thought it would be more successful using racism as their primary goal because most Americans would agree with fighting against that. They formed the group Anti-Racist Action or ARA, which is believed to have a direct tie to the modern group now called Antifa.

Scot Crow, a former Antifa organizer, is quoted as saying, "The idea in Antifa is that we go where they (right-wingers) go. That hate speech is not free speech. That if you are endangering people with what you say and the actions that are behind them, then you do not have the right to do that. And so we go to cause conflict, to shut them down where they are because we don't believe that Nazis or fascists of any stripe should have a mouthpiece."

The media accused Antifa of throwing molotov cocktails and breaking windows during the 2017 Berkeley protests while Milo Yiannopoulos (an alt-right provocateur) was speaking. It was rumored that Antifa might have been the cause of the Rose Parade in 2017 being canceled because of threats of violence and shutting down streets as a direct result of members of the republican party being in the parade. Many other events were canceled either by threat or by actions of violence during 2017 that had to do with right-wing thinking.

As with the current acceptance of socialism and communism by our youth due to professors teaching those ideas, you will find many college groups sympathizing with and even wanting to join Antifa to help accomplish their goal to defeat fascism.

The use of violence was clearly seen in 2018 at the event, "A Night for Freedom" held by the far-right in Manhattan. They used intimidation by putting 1,595 ICE officials' pictures and names out so the group can know who they are. This is information that Antifa is probably going to use it to attack these people. They have also used intimidation tactics on others stating, "We know where you sleep at night."

Statements like that above are no doubt terrorist statements and also should be considered hate statements, but it's funny how the far-left can get away with making such statements. According to 6 USCS § 101, the term terrorism is "any activity that--

(A) involves an act that--(i) is dangerous to human life or potentially destructive of critical infrastructure or key resources; and (ii) is a violation of the criminal laws of the United States or of any State or other subdivision of the United States; and (B) appears to be intended-- (i) to intimidate or coerce a civilian population; (ii) to influence the policy of a government by intimidation or coercion; or (iii) to affect the conduct of a government by mass destruction, assassination, or kidnapping."

Yep, I think terrorist is the right word to use for Antifa!

We might not know much about the group, but we do know they fight against authoritarianism, and fascism. This, in part, is what most Americans are against. Most Americans are against racism, Nazi ideas, dictatorship, and the like. What amazes me, however, is Antifa is sympathetic toward communism and socialism, which generally leads to totalitarianism and censorship.

They also fight against capitalism, which is what made this nation great. They look at capitalism as a way for rich people to get rich off the backs of poor people. They view it as an unfair practice because some live in luxury and others in poverty.

What they fail to realize is that in America everyone has the right, as we have said before, to become whatever they want to be. They, like most people who support socialism and communism, think that if our nation goes that direction, all will have the same. They, to me, are lazy and looking for the easy way out. They want someone else to take care of them. Personally, I believe our government has helped bring this ideology about with all the free programs we have. We now have what is called three generations of welfare recipiency. The welfare system was never meant for that purpose. It was created to help people for a short amount of time during hardship. Our government is now taking this a step further by allowing illegals welfare and free health care.

Antifa is also against the far-right, classifying almost all of us as fascists and capitalists in its negative form of controlling all the money by an elite group of people, and that is simply not the case. Just because I may have strong moral values or have a strong religious faith doesn't make me a hater of those that oppose it. It is my right to believe homosexuality is wrong, but at the same time, it is your right to think there is nothing wrong with it.

It is because of the intimidations and name-calling that keep the majority of Americans that have a high-moral belief system quiet. Their actions actually look more like authoritarianism than those of us with our traditional American ideas.

To order other books from this author, go to:
www.treeoflifecoaching.org

Chapter 10

COVID-19—Pandemic or Power Control

Just when you thought it was safe to go back outside because of the riots and looting…Here comes COVID-19!

There have been many conspiracy theories about the COVID-19 virus. Many think it is a biological warfare virus that was made by China, and it escaped accidentally. Some say it is so the World Health Organization (WHO) can get money, and some of our elite, wealthy people who are in the pharmaceutical business are set to make a fortune. Still, others believe it is a hoax so the government can take full control of our lives, thus taking over our country.

The one thing that is sure is that we don't know much about the virus other than it came from China, and it is much like other COVID viruses but without a vaccination. And as we will soon see, there is more than meets the eye than what is being said.

As far as we can tell, the virus seemed to have started in Wuhan, China, back in November of 2019. Since that time, there have been almost 20 million cases report worldwide, most of which are very mild. There also have been reported over 700,000 deaths worldwide.

These numbers are alarming for sure, but we must look further to see how these numbers are derived.
In the United States (at the time of writing this section of the book, which is August 11, 2020), there have been 5,182,177 cases reported with 165,286 deaths, according to the CDC. The American people are in a panic!

To make it more alarming to the American people, the virus was declared a public health emergency of international concern on January 30, 2020 by the WHO (World Health Organization). By March 11, 2020, it was upgraded to a pandemic.

At the very beginning of this virus, my intuition said something was not right. I had a strange feeling inside that the government was hiding something from the American people and had another plan in mind. Although this may not be able to be proven at the moment, still, there are warning signs that people need to heed and watch very closely. Typically, once a person realizes it was a conspiracy, it's too late, the damage has already been done.

According to the WHO and the CDC, the virus incubation time is anywhere from one to fourteen days. Because of this, the CDC has asked people, and at times forced people, to self-quarantine. They say that the virus can stay alive for up to four hours on copper but up to three days on plastic. Think of that before you grab your next bottle of soda or water!

One of the first things that brought suspicion to my mind was that the WHO only recommended people space themselves 3 feet apart while the CDC recommended 6 feet apart. That is a pretty big difference in distance. You would think that a World Health Organization would know more about the virus and what to do than the CDC. As I said, conspiracies are hard to prove, so this one may just be that the CDC wants the U.S. to take more caution than the rest of the world.

Another conspiracy is that the virus has been created to help deplete the black, brown, and Indian populations. Although it is true that it appears that more blacks, browns, and Indians contract the virus, the cause is not a conspiracy against them, and the virus itself doesn't know the difference in race.

So what is causing it to hit those minorities more than others? There are a couple of factors that are probably the cause. First, many people in the minority bracket live in very close proximity to others, which makes the spread of the virus more easily accomplished. Also, during the pandemic, you can see on the news many minorities are protesting in tight quarters all over the United States. Many of those are not wearing masks, and there is still a debate on just how effective the masks are.

Another reason is that many of these neighborhoods sponsor block parties, which once again involves a large number of people not taking the precautions needed during this pandemic.

One other thing that could partly be the cause is, for some God awful reason, our youth have taken a challenge to be around someone that is infected with the virus and not take any precautions as a dare. It just shows the mindset of many of the youths that are out protesting today and the lack of common sense they have.

And finally, many minorities, like other poor people, have to take public transportation or have bad health problems, and can't afford insurance. Combined, all of these can be a significant factor as well.

Cases began to multiply in the United States, and by March 15, 2020, the CDC recommended no gatherings over 50 people for an eight week period to help slow the virus down. On March 16th, President Trump changed the guidelines to 10 people or less and asked people to avoid traveling if possible. These restrictions were forecasted to last until August, which caused the Federal Reserve Bank to lower rates and the stock market to slide because of the fear of a recession.

Because of the spread of the virus, many doctors and people in the medical field sent letters asking ICE to release people that were detained for immigration violations, due to overcrowding. (Why not deport them as should be done)?

Even after the White House lifted restrictions, many state and local governments continued to have strict guidelines for business and the public on what they can and can't do. Restrictions continue, from a wearing a mask everywhere you go, to businesses, schools having virtual classes instead of in-person, and restricting numbers in gatherings including churches and restaurants.

At one time there was talk, and still could be implemented, of making the entire nation take a vaccine. If you decided not to take the vaccine, you might not be able to go back to your job, or shop, or go in public. They also are pushing that all Americans get a vaccine once it becomes available for the COVID-19 virus.

To make things even more interesting, I wonder if you knew that without you downloading it or adding an app to your phone, a new function had been installed. It is the COVID-19 Exposure Notifications App.

Basically, this app, when turned on, will alert you when someone that has been diagnosed with COVID-19 is near you. Not only have they developed this app, which to me, is secretly gathering data and information about you, but they also have supplied a number where you can call and report people who are not wearing masks!

This might not seem alarming to you, and you may feel this is for the safety of the people, but don't be fooled. This is a systemic way of getting you used to reporting people and monitoring everything you do.

Because of the shutdown and restrictions, people are losing their jobs, businesses are shutting down, and our economy is heading toward a recession. All the while, the government is sending out unemployment checks, which in some cases, are giving more money to stay home than people made when they worked, and also giving stimulus checks to everyone making a certain amount of money or less.

They had given this bailout money before to companies that were failing, such as the airline and car industries. So, isn't this a good thing? Not really!

The whole purpose of capitalism is people must produce to make it. If a business fails, another person will step up to grow a new idea or business that will be successful. It is the freedom to build a business or work for a company that makes this nation great and prosperous. It is not the government's job to get into the private sector and use our tax dollars to bail a failed business out. Most of the time, the business failed because of poor management and not making proper financial decisions. The government, in my opinion, shouldn't have shut all this down to begin with. Distance, sanitary conditions, and masks should have done just as well.

Besides that, all the money is the government is spending is money we don't have. Before all of the problems we have had these past four years, we have hardly been able just to pay the interest on loans we have from other countries. How are we then thinking we can afford to borrow more? It doesn't take a rocket scientist to figure out you can't borrow from Peter to pay Paul. Sooner or later, YOU WILL GO BROKE! But that might just be the whole purpose of spending all this money. It is an advantage to big governments when money fails. It is at that time they can deem your current form of money worthless and develop another type of currency that they can control.

You might think that talking about them changing the money for their advantage, making us take vaccines, and keeping a tab on us as part of a plan is a conspiracy theory, but trust me, communists have used all of the above to take down a country before.

Don't get me wrong. I believe the COVID-19 is a dangerous virus and can be deadly, but it has been manipulated to be far much worse than it is. For instance, I know personally of people who have been told they tested positive for the virus who never took the test! How can that be?

Furthermore, the CDC has even admitted to fudging on the numbers. And did you know that if a doctor reports a patient as having COVID-19, he is paid large sums of money as well as calling a death COVID-19 no matter if it may have actually been due to heart failure? That's right, up to three times more money. All you have to do is follow the money to see the truth.

Speaking of money, the president at first was praising the result of hydroxychloroquine and zinc. Immediately, the public was told it was not a cure and could even cause death. It is now almost impossible to get hydroxychloroquine in the United States. This is a very cheap drug, and in many places around the world, it is over-the-counter medicine.

Although the main spokesmen for the COVID-19 pandemic said it didn't work, hundreds of doctors and nurses have addressed the White House stating that it was successful in many of their patients. Could it be that because hydroxychloroquine, which is very cheap and the alternative drugs being used by the COVID-19 cost as high as $3,500 a dose be a factor in its effectiveness?

In a televised briefing, the Illinois Department of Public Health Director, Dr. Ngozi Ezike with knowledge of COVID-19 and its guidelines, gave the following statement defining a COVID-19 death. "At the time of death, um, it was a COVID positive diagnosis, so that means if you were in hospice and had already been given a few weeks to live, and then you were also found to have COVID, that would be counted as a COVID death. It means that if um, technically that even if you died of of a clear alternate cause, but you have COVID at the same time, it's still listed as a COVID death. So, um, everyone that is listed as a COVID death doesn't mean that COVID was the cause of the death, but they had COVID at the time of death."

According to that definition, a man can be run over by a bus, die from falling off a mountain, or have his head cut off, but if he also had COVID at the time, it is counted as a COVID death. Listen people, it's a person dies who is 90 years old with heart problems but also has COVID, the cause of death is heart failure. Get the picture? You are being lied to and misled for a purpose.

And let's also look at things that happened in the past that didn't cause all this chaos. Although these numbers, most of them very distorted, sound alarming, the fact is, the common flu at times has had over 250,000-500,000 deaths worldwide, according to the World Health Organization. The CDC says an estimate of 9.2 to 35 million people will contract the flu with as many as 700,000 dying each year.

And when it came to the bird flu of 2009, an estimated 1.4 billion of mild cases were reported and could have caused, according to WHO, up to 575,000 deaths. So, why weren't any of those cause for a shutdown? It is my opinion, it wasn't the right time for a crisis situation. And for the record, wasn't it funny that while the BLM and ANTIFA were making news with riots and looting, COVID-19 took a backseat until the crisis calmed down some? Now, COVID-19 is back on top.

If you think you are not being played, think again. This pandemic has cost jobs, kept people away from their churches and loved ones, and caused our leaders to wield their power to tell you where you will go and how you will go. This is a way to normalize the control the government has on you and, once again, fooling the people to believe it is for their own good and protection. And by the way, in the next section, I hope to deal with what all the fuss is about to have everyone vaccinated. You might be shocked at the real reason.

Chapter 11

The New World Order

If Americans ever believed there was a conspiracy going on instead of facts, it's probably the theory of a New World Order. The very idea that there are elites all over the world who are planning a global takeover is a joke to most people. They believe that because America is number one, she is too strong to take over They also think that we are too wealthy to take over. They mistakenly think our government leaders would stop such a thing. But they are very much mistaken.

The idea of a New World Order has been around as far as I am concerned, since the early 1700s. Truth be known, it was prophesied with outstanding accuracy thousands of years ago. We will go a little further on the prophecy in the next chapter.

It shouldn't be a shock that the success of this global takeover will be the result of the same measures the communists have used to take over other countries. It is mainly through finance, education, religion, and equality.

It is hard to convince people that this is not a conspiracy, but when you see the signs of the times and things that the global community is pushing toward, it takes little effort to see there is a larger picture they are striving for. I just want to give you some food for thought so you can decide for yourself, fact or theory. I will also give you quotes from some of the most influential people in the world who supporting this movement.

Here are the seven steps to make a New World Order. Ironically, Marxs had ten steps, and seven of these are included here; 1. abolish all other governments, 2. abolish private property (take away from those that have and give to those that don't), 3. to do away with family inheritance, which once again is a distribution of wealth, 4. to do away with patriotism and make it appear as unsympathetic and selfish, 5. to destroy the family and any values that tie to a family unit, 6. to do away with religion or make a substitute universal type of religion. 7. And finally, setting up a New World Government. Did I not say it follows the same guidelines as communism?

Surprisingly enough, the goals of the United Nations sounds as if they are the spearhead of a New World Government. I want to highlight some of the things that are taken from the United Nations Sustainable Development Goals knowledge platform held in New York on September 25-27 of 2015. Note; they want all of this done by 2030.

" We are determined to take the bold and transformative steps which are urgently needed to shift the world onto a sustainable and resilient path. As we embark on this collective journey, we pledge that no one will be left behind. The 17 Sustainable Development Goals and 169 targets which we are announcing today demonstrate the scale and ambition of this **_new universal_** agenda."

Even the wording gives me chills when I understand the full impact of what they are doing by trying to make our world one nation. I would hope that you visit the site called Agenda21 and read all of the actual document.

Of course, the main goal is to end poverty, hunger, promote equality, and a healthy environment. All of this sounds magnificent at first glance, but what is the hidden agenda?

Well, first of all, when they are talking about saving the planet, they are talking about things like the "Green Deal." They use global warming as their base reason something must be done now. The truth is, the Earth has always gone through changes. The Earth goes through these changes to bring balance to the system when it's out, and at times, global warming is one of those necessary things to bring the balance. But the main problem I have, to complete their goal on global warming, they must be in control of every business and production in the entire world. This will give them a global power to run everything when it comes to production. That is a freedom Americans shouldn't want to turn over to a global organization. If you control the businesses, you control the money.

Under the introduction of prosperity, it reads like this. "We are determined to ensure that all human beings can enjoy prosperous and fulfilling lives and that economic, social, and technological progress occurs in harmony with nature." Once again, in order to do this, they must have control of all finances and technology as well as what our society is taught.

And again, in the opening statement under partnership, it reads like this, "We are determined to mobilize the means required to implement this Agenda through a revitalized Global Partnership for Sustainable Development, based on a spirit of strengthened global solidarity, focused in particular on the needs of the poorest and most vulnerable and with the participation of all countries, all stakeholders, and all people. The interlinkages and integrated nature of the Sustainable Development Goals are of crucial importance in ensuring that the purpose of the new Agenda is realized. If we realize our ambitions across the full extent of the Agenda, the lives of all will be profoundly improved, and our world will be transformed for the better."

To me, this is as plain as black and white. Their ultimate goal is to have a One World Government and be able to control everyone in the world with what they feel is right. This will affect our jobs, our pay, our way of living, our freedom, our religion, our independence, our military, our police, our freedom of thought and expression, and so much more. But remember, they are doing this for the good of ALL people. However, I still believe with ultimate power comes ultimate corruption. There is no check and balance here. And for the record, their goal is impossible. There will never be a time where everyone can enjoy prosperity, peace, and free of disease and want. Well, I say never, but in the next chapter there may be a time of 3 ½ years that all of this will happen.

I said already that I believe this New World Order will come from the United Nations and I still do, but however it starts, there have been significant players pushing for the New World Government, and as promised, I just want to give facts so I will quote some of these so you can see for yourself, this is not a joke nor a conspiracy but a plan to bring this One World System to fruition.

"I am a most unhappy man. I have unwittingly ruined my country. A great industrial nation is controlled by its system of credit. Our system of credit is concentrated. The growth of the nation, therefore, and all our activities are in the hands of a few men. We have come to be one of the worst ruled, one of the most completely controlled and dominated governments in the civilized world. No longer a government by free opinion, no longer a government by conviction and the vote of the majority, but a government by the opinion and duress of a small group of dominant men." This statement was made in 1916 by President Woodrow Wilson as he was reflecting the problem that came three years earlier from him signing in the Federal Reserve Act into law. Why would that be a problem? Well, read on!

In order to understand why he was so upset, we must see what is so dangerous about the Federal

Reserve. The name itself is misleading because it is neither. Instead, it is a privately owned institution. It originated in a secret meeting back in 1910 by a group of bankers and politicians. The result of the law gave the power our government had to create money to this private group. So, if nothing else, we have proved that our financial system hangs on a few and not our government. Thus, it now can be a world banking system of international bankers and industrialists.

Louis McFaddenmember, a Republician member of the House at the time, quoted, "When the Federal Reserve Act was passed, the people of these United States did not perceive that a world banking system was being set up here. A super-state controlled by International Bankers and international industrialists acting together to enslave the world for their own pleasure. Every effort has been made by the Fed to conceal its powers, but the truth is – the Fed has usurped the Government. It controls everything here, and it controls all our foreign relations. It makes and breaks governments at will." Woodrow Wilson confirmed it by saying, " Some of the biggest men in the United States, in the field of commerce and manufacture, are afraid of something. They know that there is a power somewhere so organized, so subtle, so watchful, so interlocked, so complete, so pervasive, that they had better not speak above their breath when they speak in condemnation of it."

Albert Einstein was quoted as saying, "The only real step toward world government is world government itself." Robert F. Kennedy admitted we should strive for a New World Order as well as Richard Nixon.

Listen to this quote by David Rockefeller. The Rockefellers have, for a long time, been speculated to be a part of the One World System goal. Here it not only proves it but shows how they plan on bringing it about, and we see it today! "We are on the verge of a global transformation. All we need is the right major crisis, and the nations will accept the New World Order."

Henry Kissinger has often promoted the plan for a New World Order. He also admitted that NAFTA was a major step toward the New World Order. NAFTA deals with our trading system.

Fidel Castro, in 1979 at the United Nations, demanded a New World Order. Michail Gorbachev also pushed for a New World Order.

Here is a direct quote from George Bush "Now, we can see a new world coming into view. A world in which there is the very real prospect of a New World Order." In the words of Winston Churchill, "A world order in which the principles of justice and fair play ... protect the weak against the strong ... A world where the United Nations, freed from cold war stalemate, is poised to fulfill the historic vision of its founders. A world in which freedom and respect for human rights find a home among all nations."

I also wanted to share a quote from Henry Kissinger he made concerning the United Nations during the Bilderberger Conference in France in 1991. "Today, America would be outraged if U.N. troops entered Los Angeles to restore order [referring to the 1991 LA riot]. Tomorrow they will be grateful! This is especially true if they were told that there were an outside threat from beyond [i.e., an "extraterrestrial" invasion], whether real or *promulgated* [emphasis mine], that threatened our very existence. It is then that all peoples of the world will plead to deliver them from this evil. The one thing every man fears is the unknown. When presented with this *scenario*, individual rights will be willingly relinquished for the guarantee of their well-being granted to them by the World Government."

The billionaire George Soros has also been identified as one that supports the idea of a One World Order. For the record, Soros hates America and has sworn to defeat her. Here is what he said at the World Affairs Council Press Conference in 1994, "[The New World Order] cannot happen without U.S. participation, as we are the most significant single component. Yes, there will be a New World Order, and it will force the United States to change its perceptions."

Nelson Mandela also embraced the thought of a New World Order and Gen. Colin Powell, in a statement in 1993, openly admitted there is a plan for a New World Order when he was talking about pulling troops out of Somalia saying it would be, and I quote, "devastating to our hopes for the New World Order and our ability to participate in multinational organizations to deal with problems like this." Inquirer (October 1994)

I think these well-known world leaders, as well as military, financial and peace leaders, are enough proof there is a plan to bring out a New World Order. These are direct quotes, not hearsay. There are other supporters like Bill Clinton, Bernie Sanders, and

Barak Obama, but we will stop here so we can move on.

Adolf Hitler said during WWII how this New World Order would come about. "National Socialism will use its own revolution for establishing a New World Order."

America, and its values and freedoms have long stood in the way of communism and a One World Order; however, even as far back as 2014 from an article entitled "Here's our 70 Socialist Congressmen," there was a list of 70 democratic socialists in our congress.

Don't be fooled, there is nothing different about democratic socialist and communist. It is the socialists and communists who are hell-bent on bringing a New World Order so ALL nations can be completely controlled by these elites. Before you vote in 2020 and anytime thereafter (if we still have the right to vote), check to see who is for socialism and vote them out for the sake of our country and our freedom.

Chapter 12

One Nation Under G~~o~~d

Most people in America know that this nation was sought out by our forefathers so that they would be able to worship God as they saw fit. Even while forming our government and laws, they quoted the Bible over 15,000 times. When they were in session, they would open and close in prayer. It is obvious they felt that God and what His Word said was to be the building block to a free society, and the Word should be used as a guideline for our values and laws.

The whole meaning of the "separation between church and state" was to keep the government from forming a church. And yet today, our government is doing it's best to interfere with churches and their belief. One of the best examples is them trying to force fundamental protestant churches to allow homosexuals to be church leaders. This is absolutely against the very Bible the protestants preach from.

Article 1 of the U.S. Bill of Rights, I repeat, is supposed to guard our religious freedom. "Congress shall make no law respecting an establishment of religion, or prohibiting the free exercise thereof; or abridging the freedom of speech, or of the press; or the right of the people peaceably to assemble, and to petition the government for a redress of grievances."

Religion is what brings our morals and values. Without them, mankind heads to a downward spiral of evil and hatred. George Washington once said, "Religion and morality are the essential pillars of civil society."

John Adams said, "Suppose a nation in some distant region should take the Bible for their only law Book, and every member should regulate his conduct by the precepts there exhibited! Every member would be obliged in conscience, to temperance, frugality, and industry; to justice, kindness, and charity towards his fellow men; and to piety, love, and reverence toward Almighty God ... What a Eutopia, what a Paradise would this region be."

Most all of the founding fathers were Christians and held fast to the Christian faith values. Most believed in Jesus Christ, God the Father, and the Holy Spirit. Benjamin Franklin made it clear concerning his faith when he said, "Here is my creed. I believe in one God, the Creator of the universe. That He governs it by His providence. That He ought to be worshipped.

The first time the phrase "In God we Trust" was engraved on our money was in 1864 on a 2- cent coin, and since has on our paper money since 1957. President Dwight D. Eisenhower approved the motto in 1956, which was the year it was authorized and signed to be on all paper money and coins through public law.

Part of the original national anthem that Francis Scott Key wrote said, "And this be our motto: In God is our trust. And the Star-Spangled Banner in triumph shall wave, O'er the land of the free and the home of the brave."

Our Pledge of Allegiance to our flag didn't have God mentioned in it in the beginning. It was first written so that any nation could use it as their pledge. It was originally written as, "I pledge allegiance to my flag and the republic, for which it stands,—one nation, indivisible—with liberty and justice for all."

But because of the fear of communism taking over, President Dwight Eisenhower thought it essential to add "under God" as a distinction between America and the rest of the world. So today, our pledge is as follows, "I pledge allegiance to the flag of the United States of America, and to the republic for which it stands, one nation under God, indivisible, with liberty and justice for all." It is too bad that most schools don't open with the Pledge of Allegiance as they did in the past and that our government is even trying to stop us from flying our flag.

It is without a doubt that the socialists and communists of this nation are taking away our religious freedom because they know the power it brings to the people. It is also setting us up for the "New World Order."

I had mentioned Antonio Gramsci's plan. He was a dedicated Marxist and started a paper called The New Order. He wanted to destroy the Christian belief because he had seen that the more people attacked Christianity, it became stronger.

So he devised the plan to attack society's belief and moral system subtly to conquer Christianity by controlling the churches, education, news, music, and arts. He believed communism would then be able to control human thought. This, in turn, would make the resistors love their servitude.

He accomplished his goal by changing churches to political clubs that focused on social justice and worship became no more than entertainment. No longer were morality and values taught.

He not only removed the past from education but also dumbed it down and started what we now know as being politically correct. He used the media to help destroy morality by harassing and discrediting traditional values and those who practiced it. Anything that was moral, decent, or had old virtues was ridiculed. And the sanctity of marriage was downplayed. His plan worked, and it is working today!

The Bible told of an age where even the church would fall asleep. It described how people would not be able to withstand true doctrine but would search for leaders who would tell them God is going to bless them no matter what they do. We see that in most of the mega-churches in America today.

Sadly, Americans can find millions of so-called preachers who, for money and fame, are selling out the true Word of God!!!! Very few preachers today will be bold enough to preach, "thus saith the Lord."

John cried out for the people to repent. Preachers in the past and today have warned about the coming persecutions. I remember as a small boy, my father teaching a Sunday School class on the book of The Revelations with a crowd of over 100 people (which in that day was a lot for a Sunday School class) and it never failed, as he was teaching what is supposed to happen, the next Sunday's newspaper would generally have the proof of it coming on the front page of the AJC (Atlanta Journal-Constitution paper. People just knew that Christ was coming back, and many made the foolish statement it would be in just a couple of years back then.

It wasn't long till people began to have a deaf ear to it, and now when we preach on the coming of Christ being near, people are not listening but instead looking at the time on their watch or thinking about what they will eat after service.

To make a statement when Christ returns is foolish because even Christ Himself doesn't know the day or the hour, but He did say we could know the season, AND THE SEASON IS HERE, CLOSER NOW THAN IT EVER HAS BEEN!!!!

IT'S TIME FOR THE BLOOD-BOUGHT
CHURCH TO GET BACK ON ITS FEET AND
WARN THIS SINFUL AND ADULTEROUS
GENERATION ON WHAT IS ABOUT TO COME
AS FAR AS JUDGEMENT ON AMERICA!!!!

Never in all of history have all the things needed
for the fulfillment of the prophesies to be completed
been in place as they are now.

It was told, two witnesses would be slain and the
WHOLE WORLD would see it. With the internet,
live streaming, satellites, and our technology, it is
possible to see it immediately as it unfolds.

It foretold of a day the money would fail. We see
it come to pass now. It won't be long because of the
mass money our government spends that
hyperinflation is going to hit and the money will
become useless.

It was foretold that Israel would be surrounded by
its enemies. Only in our generation could that be
seen because only in our generation has Israel
become a nation again speaking their original LOST
language.

It was foretold that men would become lovers of themselves instead of lovers of God, that men's hearts would grow cold and hard, and that their conscience would be seared as with a hot iron.

It was foretold that moral values would decline, and what once was right would now be thought of as evil, and what was evil will be thought of as right.   We in America would never have dreamed 50 years ago, that the vast majority of Americans would agree with what is taking place now.

It's time to wake up America!!!!

The Bible speaks of a time that the whole world will be under the control of one person. I had mentioned in the previous chapter that there is coming a day when all the world will be at peace, be financially secure, and all of its problems met for a short time, mainly 3 ½ years. The Bible has prophesied that as well. A man, the "Anti-Christ," will bring these things about, but after that, the following 3 ½ years will be years of devastation like man has never seen before. As sure as I am writing this book, it will happen just as the Word of God has said.

Concerning vaccinations it was also foretold that there would be a mark placed on the forehead or right palm on everyone in the world, and without it, you wouldn't be able to buy or sell. It was told that the world would be under this one-world government. As they now push for this vaccine, they are also pushing for an ID to be inserted in the hand or forehead. It has already been developed. And amazingly, the root word for the injector is the same word used in the Bible when it was talking about this mark being placed on the forehead or palm.

Why do I and our forefathers put so much faith in the Word of God? Because the Word of God has been proven to be correct through thousands of prophecies already fulfilled.

Science has tried to dispel it as being a fairy tale. Darwin mocked creation until, one day, he finally admitted that creation was the way the earth and man were made. But just to give more validity to the Word of God, let me give you just a few things in the Scripture that science recently proved was correct but the Bible told of it thousands of years ago.

In Job 26:7, "He (God) stretcheth out the north over the empty place, and hangeth the earth upon nothing." Written in 1500 B.C., yet science didn't discover this until 1650.

Hebrews 11:3, "Through faith, we understand that the worlds were framed by the word of God, so that things which are seen were not made of things which do appear." Only recently has science found out about everything is made out of atoms, things unseen. The Bible told us this 2000 years ago!

The Book of Job, written in 1520 B.C., tells that air can be weighed. It talks of the Earth's rotation. It mentions springs being in the sea.

We credit Christopher Columbus with finding out that the world is round in the 1600s, but in Isaiah 40:22 written around 740 B.C, God said, "It is he that sitteth upon the circle of the earth, and the inhabitants thereof are as grasshoppers; that stretcheth out the heavens as a curtain, and spreadeth them out as a tent to dwell in."

2000 years before science knew that there are "cycles" in air currents, the Bible said in Ecclesiastes 1:6 "The wind goeth toward the south, and turneth about unto the north; it whirleth about continually, and the wind returneth again according to his circuits."

Time forbids me to prove the Bible through history, prophecies, archaeology, biology, and medicine. There are more found manuscripts showing the Scriptures than any other thing, including writings of Nostradamus, who lived in the 1500s.

More people believe Nostradamus, and science uses his thoughts, and yet they discredit the Bible. America can throw away the Bible and its teachings as heresies, but I can promise you, America will stand in judgment because of rejecting it.

I personally blame the church as the main reason we are in this situation. We have compromised with the world so we can have pleasures. We allow the media to mock God and destroy family values with nudity, profanity, vulgarity, and moral rebellion.

Because Christians have acted as the world and have become "Traitors, heady, highminded, lovers of pleasures, more than lovers of God" (2 Timothy 3:4), we will see God's wrath on this nation.

There are approximately 67% of people who claim to be Christians. Despite what Barak Obama says, we are still considered a mostly Christian nation, and if we as Christians boycotted this stuff, they would have to stop it.

But why don't we do that? Because we like what they are giving us! We as Christians have struck the word God out of the motto, "One Nation Under God."

John, in his day, tried to warn his people, "repent for the Kingdom of God is at hand." I will say, as he did back then, to us now in America, "REPENT FOR THE KINGDOM OF GOD IS AT HAND!!! "

So, what can we do?

You can first start by stop believing the lies and propaganda that the media is spreading.

The gays are still 4.5 percent of the nation's population, not as powerful as the media wants you to believe. Because they unite and protest and the media gives them the stage, they appear to be nearing the majority, but it is an illusion.

Regardless of what the media is trying to portray, many blacks and whites still care deeply about each other, and many treasure each other's friendship. Most of our policemen are honest, hard-working, law-abiding people. Most of the people still believe in God and His principles. Most gun owners are good, law-abiding citizens that pose no threat. Most religions may condemn a behavior but still love the person that has the unacceptable behavior. Don't fall for this stupid thinking where they are trying to divide us as a Nation.

Luke 11:17 (KJV)

17 But he, knowing their thoughts, said unto them, Every kingdom divided against itself is brought to desolation; and a house divided against a house falleth.

We must unite in our thinking and get back to our grass roots of this country if we are to survive.

You might say, "Roger, you are just paranoid. None of this has any real meaning. We are doing just fine as a nation, and nothing will ever take us over."

Let me share these instructions in a secret document, allegedly authored by the Communist International for their "young revolutionaries." The document is titled "Rules of Revolution":

1. Corrupt the young, get them interested in sex, take them away from religion. Make them superficial and enfeebled.

2. Divide the people into hostile groups by constantly harping on controversial issues of no importance.

3. Destroy people's faith in their national leaders by holding the latter up for contempt, ridicule, and disgrace.

4. Always preach democracy, but seize power as fast and as ruthlessly as possible.

5. By encouraging government extravagances, destroy its credit, produce years of inflation with rising prices, and general discontent.

6. Incite unnecessary strikes in vital industries, encourage civil disorders, and foster a lenient and soft attitude on the part of the government towards such disorders.

7. Cause breakdown of the old moral virtues: honesty, sobriety, self-restraint, faith in the pledged word.

Does it sound like America today? You better wake from your sleep.

So is there any hope?

The election in 2020 might just be the last time that America is free to vote. I fear we are too far gone, and God's judgment now is against this nation, but as with every one of the believers before us, we must not give up.

Pray harder than you have ever prayed for God to send a revival. Pray first that God will cleanse you and revive you with a new zeal to serve Him with all your heart, mind, and strength.

Pray for God to give you direction on what your part should be in all of this.

Then write your government leaders and let them know your stance and your beliefs, and that you want them to protect your rights. Look into your representatives' voting record to find out what they stand for. Read the laws that are being passed with hidden items in them. Educate yourself and VOTE!

According to most people who have lived under communist rule, they feel the only way to take this country back is by brute force. I personally do not suggest that even if it may be true, but I can't rule out that it may come to just that.

Remember, we are not of this world or its government. Our home and government is led by the King of Kings and Lord of Lords, and our homeland has not been made by human hands.

We have been sent here to be a light in this dark world. BE THAT LIGHT EVEN IN YOUR DARKEST HOUR. Be like John, a voice in the wilderness crying "repent for the kingdom of God is at hand."

Start a small group of friends that you can talk to and discuss problems and also be able to get encouragement from when you feel weak.

READ YOUR BIBLE!!! "Thy word have I hid in mine hear,t that I might not sin against thee." Ps. 119:11

And most of all, don't walk in fear. God knows the situation, and with all the chaos, He is allowing things to happen to fit His plan already spoken in His Word. GODS GOT THIS!!!! He will give you the grace to walk through whatever is to come our way.

It is my hope this book will open the eyes of some people before this nation is overtaken. Even if it is overtaken, and I am killed because of my faith and the tribulation period starts, maybe there will be some of the DVDs around so some people may hear the truth and be saved.

I want to close with this thought, which is a part of the book entitled "Little Rope, Big Elephant."

In India, a man observed a child with a rope tied to his ankle and the other end of the rope tied to a huge elephant. The man couldn't believe that such a small child could keep that huge elephant from running away, so he asked a villager how could that be possible.

The villager told the traveler, when an elephant is born and is very small, they tie him to the rope with an anchor strong enough to keep the elephant contained in a small area.

The small elephant every day would pull hard to get away but with no success. As time goes by, the elephant then quits trying because, in his head, he cannot escape.

It is then we can contain the elephant with the rope tied to the smallest object, and he will not try and escape.

Our government and people in this nation are trying to make us believe we have no power to escape what is going on, but I want you to know, we have the most power available in the universe if we will only turn back to it. That power is in our God and His Son Jesus Christ.

If we repent and God allows revival to break out in this country one more time, we will defeat the enemy that is trying to destroy us and keep us from waking from our sleep.

WAKE UP AND LET'S TAKE AMERICA BACK!

www.ingramcontent.com/pod-product-compliance
Lightning Source LLC
Chambersburg PA
CBHW060835110426
R18122100001BA/R181221PG42736CBX00034BA/41